To

Desi

From

Mom & Dad

Date

Happy Easter! 2015

VeggieTales

GROWING Day By Day

365 DAILY DEVOS for BOYS

© 2015 Big Idea Entertainment, LLC. All Rights Reserved.

ISBN 978-1-61795-518-1

Published by Worthy Kids, an imprint of Worthy Publishing Group, a division of Worthy Media, Inc. 134 Franklin Road, Suite 200, Brentwood, Tennessee 37027.

Scripture references marked KJV are from the Holy Bible, King James Version.

Scripture references marked NKJV are from the Holy Bible, New King James Version. Copyright © 1982 by Thomas Nelson, Inc. Used by permission.

Scripture references marked NIV are from the Holy Bible, New International Version®. Copyright © 1973, 1978, 1984, 2011 International Bible Society. Used by permission of Zondervan. All rights reserved.

Scripture references marked NLT are from the Holy Bible, New Living Translation. Copyright © 1996 Tyndale Charitable Trust. Used by permission of Tyndale House Publishers.

Scripture references marked NCV are from the New Century Version®. Copyright © 1987, 1988, 1991 by Word Publishing, a division of Thomas Nelson, Inc. All rights reserved. Used by permission.

Scripture references marked HCSB are from the Holman Christian Standard Bible™. Copyright © 1999, 2000, 2001 by Holman Bible Publishers. Used by permission.

Scripture references marked NASB are from the New American Standard Bible®. Copyright © 1960, 1962, 1963, 1968, 1971, 1972, 1973, 1975, 1977, 1995 by The Lockman Foundation. Used by permission.

Scripture references marked ESV are from the Holy Bible, English Standard Version. The Holy Bible, English Standard Version. Copyright © 2001 by Crossway Bibles, a division of Good News Publishers.

Scripture references marked TLB are from the Holy Bible, The Living Bible, Copyright © 1971 owned by assignment by Illinois Regional Bank N.A. (as trustee). Used by permission of Tyndale House Publishers, Inc., Wheaton, Illinois 60189. All rights reserved.

Scripture references marked MSG are from the Holy Bible, The Message - This edition issued by contractual arrangement with NavPress, a division of The Navigators, U.S.A. Originally published by NavPress in English as THE MESSAGE: The Bible in Contemporary Language copyright 2002-2003 by Eugene Peterson. All rights reserved.

Scripture references marked GNT are from the Holy Bible, Good News Translation. Copyright © 1992 American Bible Society. All rights reserved. Used by permission.

Scripture references marked CEV are from the Holy Bible, Contemporary English Version.® Copyright © 1995 American Bible Society. All rights reserved.

Scripture references marked ICB are from the Holy Bible, International Children's Bible®, New Century Version®. Copyright © 1986, 1988, 1999 by Tommy Nelson™, a division of Thomas Nelson, Inc. All rights reserved. Used by permission.

Cover Design and Page Layout by Bart Dawson

VeggieTales

GROWING
Day by Day

365 DAILY DEVOS for BOYS

a message to Parents

If you're already a fan of VeggieTales®, you know the importance of teaching your son the big ideas that are found in God's Holy Word. And this book of devotions can help you do just that.

This text (which is intended to be read by Christian parents to their young children) contains 365 brief chapters, one for each day of the year. Each chapter contains kid-friendly essays on important topics such as honesty, generosity, forgiveness, and kindness.

During the coming year, try this experiment: read a chapter from this book every day. When you do, you'll have 365 different opportunities to share God's love and His wisdom with your son, and that's a good thing . . . a very good thing.

Starting Your Day

This is the day the Lord has made; let us rejoice and be glad in it.

Psalm 118:24 HCSB

Each new day is a gift from God and getting it off to a good start is a really great idea.

How do you begin your day? Your mom has probably told you how important it is to have a good breakfast. Getting enough sleep the night before is a big help, too. Waking up in time to get ready for whatever you have to do can make things better.

But you might not know how important it is to remember to thank God for the new day He has made for you. It's a wonderful way to start your day!

THOUGHT OF THE DAY

When you get up in the morning, sing your favorite song from church.

PRAY TODAY

Dear God, thank You for this new day You have made. Thank You for loving me and being with me all day long. Amen.

FULL OF HOPE

May the God of hope fill you with all joy and peace as you trust in him, so that you may overflow with hope by the power of the Holy Spirit.

Romans 15:13 NIV

Hope is a wonderful thing to have . . . and to share. Hope can change everything and everyone for the better.

How can you have hope? Trust God to help you think good thoughts and believe the best. Become best friends with Jesus. Read the Bible and learn what God says is true. Don't pay attention to fear and never give up.

Then, when you've filled your heart with God's hope and gladness, share your hopeful thoughts with your friends and family. They will be blessed, and so will you.

THOUGHT OF THE DAY

When you are having a hard day, close your eyes and think of something that God has done for you.

PRAY TODAY

Dear God, thank You for all You have done for me and for giving me hope. Amen.

FOLLOW HIM

"Teacher, I will follow you wherever you go."

Matthew 8:19 ESV

Who was the greatest teacher in the history of the world? Jesus! He set the perfect example and taught us how to live, how to treat others, and how to worship God.

The more you spend time with Him by praying and reading the Bible, the more you can learn about how to live. And that learning never ends. Jesus will keep teaching you important lessons throughout your life.

Ask Jesus to teach you something today, and thank Him for loving you so much!

THOUGHT OF THE DAY

What do you think it means to follow Jesus?

PRAY TODAY

Dear God, thank You for Jesus. I am so glad that He is my teacher and that He can help me with every problem. Amen.

He Will Take Care of You

Fear of man will prove to be a snare, but whoever trusts in the Lord is kept safe.

Proverbs 29:25 NIV

The Bible tells us the story of Joseph. He had a lot of brothers who were jealous of him, and they sold him as a slave. But Joseph worked hard and God kept him safe.

Then, someone lied and Joseph was thrown in jail. But God took care of him there, too. Finally, Joseph got out of jail and saved an entire country—and his whole family, too.

How did Joseph do these things? He trusted God even when things were pretty hard. Even when you can't understand what God is doing, trust Him anyway. He will take care of you!

THOUGHT OF THE DAY

How do you think you would feel if what happened to Joseph happened to you? Could you trust God to keep you safe?

PRAY TODAY

Dear God, I don't always understand what You are doing, but I will trust You anyway. Thank You for taking care of me. Amen.

EVERYTHING IS POSSIBLE

Jesus looked at them intently, then said, "Without God, it is utterly impossible. But with God everything is possible."

Mark 10:27 TLB

Are you facing a problem too big for you to solve? The good news is God can do anything. There's no miracle that's impossible for Him to perform. There's no job too big, or too hard, for Him. Whatever the size of your problem, God is bigger. Much bigger!

Are you afraid to ask God to do something big? Don't be. Your Heavenly Father wants you to ask Him for the things you need. Everything is possible with God! All you need to do is ask for help . . . He's always ready to listen.

THOUGHT OF THE DAY

Can you think of a story in the Bible when God did the impossible?

PRAY TODAY

Dear God, I really need Your help. Thank You that no problem is too big for You! Amen.

Parents Can Help

The one who lives with integrity is righteous; his children who come after him will be happy.

Proverbs 20:7 HCSB

Whenever you want to get better at something, you can always be willing to let your parents help out in any way they can. After all, your parents want you to become the very best person you can be.

What can they help you with? Learning self-control. Being kind to others. Learning a new skill or hobby. Homework. Sharing stories about your family and heritage. Teaching you about faith in God. Pretty much anything you can imagine!

Don't be afraid to ask them for help—it's why God gave you parents!

THOUGHT OF THE DAY
Are you interested in something your parents do well? Ask them about it!

PRAY TODAY
Dear God, thank You for my parents. Give them wisdom, courage, and faith. Amen.

SHOWING RESPECT

Show respect for all people. Love the brothers and sisters of God's family.

1 Peter 2:17 ICB

Are you polite and respectful to your parents and teachers? Do you try your best to treat everybody with the respect they deserve? If you want to please God, then showing respect to others is a very important thing to do.

How do you show respect? By listening politely. By not arguing or talking back–especially with grownups. By speaking kind words and waiting your turn. By looking for the good in each person.

These are simple things, but they can make a big difference!

THOUGHT OF THE DAY

Try to find one good thing to say about every person you meet.

PRAY TODAY

Dear God, please help me do my best to show respect for everyone in my life. Amen.

in His Time

He has made everything beautiful in its time.

Ecclesiastes 3:11 NIV

Sometimes, the hardest thing to do is to wait. This is really true when we are in a big hurry and when we want things to happen right away!

Still, God always knows best. He made you and only He knows what is exactly right for you; to make you everything He intended you to be. Even though sometimes it's hard, it is always worth the wait for God's perfect timing. So, relax and wait . . . then watch what He does.

THOUGHT OF THE DAY

What are some ways you can spend your time while you are waiting?

PRAY TODAY

Dear God, sometimes I want things to happen in a hurry. But You know what's best for me, so I will wait for You. Amen.

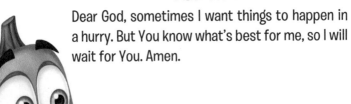

THE GIFT OF PEACE

Peace I leave with you; my peace I give you. I do not give to you as the world gives. Do not let your hearts be troubled and do not be afraid.

John 14:27 NIV

When Jesus went to be with the Father in heaven, He gave us the perfect gift: peace that stays in our hearts and goes with us wherever we go. Because of His peace, you never have to worry or be afraid. But you can't find this kind of peace anywhere else—it's only available from Jesus.

God doesn't want you to be troubled or worried. When you accept His peace by opening up your heart to Him, you will feel much better about yourself, your family, and your life. So, no matter what happens, trust God and thank Him for His peace in your heart.

THOUGHT OF THE DAY

How can you do your part to keep peace in your home?

PRAY TODAY

Dear God, I thank You for the gift of peace. Help me stay peaceful and content all the time. Amen.

CHOOSING GOOD FRIENDS

Spend time with the wise and you will become wise, but the friends of fools will suffer.

Proverbs 13:20 NCV

When you spend lots of time with someone, you start to behave like they do. That's why you should choose your friends very carefully.

If you're around kids who tell the truth and make good choices, that's a good thing. But, if you start spending time with people who make bad choices, you'll be tempted to misbehave, just like they do.

God wants you to choose friends who will make you a better person and help you do what's right. And that's what you should want to do for others, too.

THOUGHT OF THE DAY

Don't be afraid to say "no." If your friend really cares about you, they will respect your choice.

PRAY TODAY

Dear God, I want to choose good friends and also be a good friend. Thank You for helping me. Amen.

A Kind Word

How wonderful it is to be able to say the right thing at the right time!

Proverbs 15:23 TLB

How hard is it to say a kind word? Not very! Yet sometimes we get so busy that we forget to say the very things that might make other people feel better.

We should always try to say nice things to our families and friends. It is also helpful to stop and think before we say something. Kind words help; but careless, cruel words hurt. It's as simple as that.

And, when we say the right thing at the right time, we give a gift that can change someone's life.

THOUGHT OF THE DAY

Stop and think before you speak!

PRAY TODAY

Dear God, I love it when someone says a kind word to me. Please help me to do the same. Amen.

a Good Time to Pray

I cried to him for help; I praised him with songs.

Psalm 66:17 GNT

If you are feeling upset, what should you do? Well, you can talk to your parents, and there's something else you can do: pray about it.

If there is a person you don't like, you should pray for a forgiving heart. If there is something you are worried about, you should ask God to give you comfort. If something exciting and wonderful has happened, He wants to hear about that too!

As you pray more, you'll discover that God is always near and that He's always ready to hear from you. Even right now!

THOUGHT OF THE DAY
The more you talk to God, the more He will talk to you.

PRAY TODAY
Dear God, help me to remember to pray every day . . . about anything and everything. Amen.

You are Wonderful

For you created my inmost being; you knit me together in my mother's womb. I praise you because I am fearfully and wonderfully made.

Psalm 139:13-14 NIV

God knew exactly what He was doing when He made you. There's nobody else in the whole wide world who's exactly like you. You're a special one-of-a-kind treasure made in God's image!

What do you think about yourself? Do you wish you were like somebody else or do you love how God made you?

Nobody's perfect—nobody. Everyone has flaws. But don't be too hard on yourself. God loves you, and He wants you to know how amazing and wonderful you really are!

THOUGHT OF THE DAY

God's definition of "beautiful" is the only one that is true.

PRAY TODAY

Dear God, thank You for making me and loving me just the way I am. Help me to love myself, too. Amen.

a Light in the Darkness

Jesus spoke to them again, saying, "I am the light of the world. He who follows Me shall not walk in darkness, but have the light of life."

John 8:12 NKJV

Have you ever been in a room that is really, really dark, and then, suddenly, someone lights a candle or turns on a flashlight? Everything changes and the darkness disappears, because even a small light can make a really big difference. It might even hurt your eyes for a moment!

That's what happens when we meet Jesus. Sometimes the world we live in can be really, really dark. But once we meet Jesus, the light comes on and the darkness disappears! Ask Him to be your Light wherever you go!

THOUGHT OF THE DAY

Turn on a small flashlight in a totally dark room. What does this tell you about the power of light?

PRAY TODAY

Dear God, I know that You sent Jesus to be the Light of the world. Help me do my best to follow Him forever. Amen.

No Excuses

Admit your faults to one another and pray for each other so that you may be healed.

James 5:16 TLB

What is an excuse? Well, when you make up an excuse, that means that you try to come up with a good reason for something you did that was wrong. Everybody makes excuses sometimes, and everyone makes mistakes. But watch out—trying to get out of trouble by making excuses all the time can just lead to more trouble.

The best way is to admit you made a mistake. So the next time you're tempted to make up an excuse, don't! Instead, just admit you were wrong. You might be amazed at the difference it can make.

THOUGHT OF THE DAY

It's a lot harder to make up excuses than to just admit you messed up!

PRAY TODAY

Dear God, when I'm tempted to make excuses, help me be strong and accept responsibility for my actions. Amen.

amazing angels

For he orders his angels to protect you wherever you go.

Psalm 91:11 TLB

Have you ever wondered if angels are real? The Bible tells us that angels come from God and they do really important things for Him. In fact, one of their most important jobs is to watch over you and keep you safe, because you matter to God!

There are lots of stories in the Bible about angels. Laura Carrot's favorite story is about an angel named Gabriel who went to tell Mary she was going to give birth to Jesus. Remember . . . just because you can't see them doesn't mean they aren't there!

THOUGHT OF THE DAY

What do you think Mary felt when she saw the angel Gabriel standing in front of her?

PRAY TODAY

Dear God, thank You for Your angels. And, I thank You for all the ways You protect me today and every day. Amen.

STAY CALM

Be angry, and do not sin; ponder in your own hearts on your beds, and be silent.

Psalm 4:4 ESV

When someone says or does something mean to you, it is easy to get really angry. In fact, it's normal! Everyone gets angry sometimes. It's what you do when you are angry that matters.

You might want to say or do something that you will be sorry about later. That's why the Bible tells us to "not sin" when we are angry. It's so much better to use self-control and stay calm. Jesus does not want your heart to be troubled by anger. Ask Him for the right words to say and He will help you.

THOUGHT OF THE DAY

When someone does something that makes you mad, take a deep breath, count to ten, and choose your words carefully!

PRAY TODAY

Dear God, when I start to feel angry, help me stay calm and not say something I shouldn't. Thank You for listening to me and helping me. Amen.

iT's a WoNDeRFuL Day!

Rejoice in the Lord and be glad, you righteous; sing, all you who are upright in heart!

Psalm 32:11 NIV

What is the best day to celebrate? Today! Every day can be a time for celebration if we think about all the wonderful things God has done for us and all of the good things yet to come.

God has made this day for you and He wants you to enjoy it! Don't worry about what happened yesterday, just look forward to the special surprises that God has planned for you today.

Every day is a gift from your Heavenly Father. So thank Him and be happy!

THOUGHT OF THE DAY

Take a moment to thank God for making a wonderful new day for you. Then, be sure to have fun!

PRAY TODAY

Dear God, thank You for making this wonderful, new day. Help me remember to celebrate all day long. Amen.

Be Cheerful!

A cheerful heart does good like medicine.

Proverbs 17:22 TLB

The Bible tells us that a cheerful heart is like medicine: it makes us and everyone around us feel better. Where does cheerfulness begin? It begins with choosing to be happy. And with a smile.

Can you think of something to smile about today? What about something that makes you giggle or laugh? Larry likes to sing a silly song or two when Bob needs some cheering up. But whatever makes you smile, think about that today and share some kindness and good cheer wherever you go.

THOUGHT OF THE DAY

Cheering up other people is a wonderful way to help yourself feel better, too!

PRAY TODAY

Dear God, please help me to be quick to smile today and to share Your love with my family and friends. Amen.

THE WAY THAT YOU THINK

Make your own attitude that of Christ Jesus.

Philippians 2:5 HCSB

What's an attitude? The word "attitude" means "the way that you think." You have more control over what you think than you realize.

Have you ever thought about how you think about things? That may sound a little silly, but you can choose to notice the good or positive in almost any situation.

A great way to have a great attitude is by learning about Jesus and what He said about life. When you do, you will see things differently . . . think about things differently . . . and your attitude will be more like His!

THOUGHT OF THE DAY

Has something been bothering you lately? Can you think of one or two good things that could come out of it?

PRAY TODAY

Dear God, help me have an attitude that is pleasing to You. I want to find the good in every situation. Amen.

GOD IS WATCHING

Remember that those who do good prove that they are God's children.

3 John 1:11 NLT

Even when nobody else is watching, God is. And He knows whether you've done the right thing or the wrong thing.

Your parents like to keep a really close eye on you, to keep you in line. But they can't be with you every minute of every day. But God can! So if you're tempted to misbehave when you think nobody is looking, remember this: Somebody is always watching over you–and that is your Father in heaven. And He wants you to do good!

THOUGHT OF THE DAY

Your actions speak much more loudly than your words.

PRAY TODAY

Dear God, show me the right thing to do–and help me do it–today and every day. Amen.

Helping Others

Work at getting along with each other and with God.

Hebrews 12:14 MSG

Helping others can be fun! It feels good to help people—and you'll know that what you're doing makes God happy. In fact, working together is a great way to show people how much God loves them.

When you show kindness and do your best to be helpful, you'll see that you can get more done together. You might even make some new friends! Working together is always better—so look for ways to share and help whoever needs it.

THOUGHT OF THE DAY

What ways can you help and work together with others?

PRAY TODAY

Dear God, help me find ways to be kind and helpful to others. I want them to know how much You love them. Amen.

Good Choices

But Daniel purposed in his heart that he would not defile himself. . . .

Daniel 1:8 KJV

Your life is a series of choices. From the moment you wake up in the morning until the time you go to sleep at night, you make lots of decisions–about the things you do, about the things you say, and about the thoughts you choose to think.

Even when a choice seems really hard, choosing to do what is right is always worth it. Remember, God always loves you, and He loves it when you make a good choice. One thing is for certain–if you always put God first, He will help you make the right choices.

THOUGHT OF THE DAY

Like Daniel, make a decision today to always choose what God would want you to do.

PRAY TODAY

Dear God, help me make choices that are pleasing to You. I want to follow Jesus every day. Amen.

Be Happy with What You Have

Don't set your heart on anything that is your neighbor's.

Exodus 20:17 MSG

Have you ever wanted something that belonged to somebody else? Most of us have felt like that at one time or another. But wanting something that doesn't belong to you . . . especially so badly that you can't think about anything else . . . makes God unhappy. And it will really make you unhappy, too.

God wants us to be thankful for the things we do have, even if they aren't always the newest or the coolest. It's always so much better to be happy with what you have!

THOUGHT OF THE DAY

If you have your heart set on something that isn't yours, make a list of your five favorite things that you do have, and thank God for those things!

PRAY TODAY

Dear God, You know the things I have been wanting. Please help me be happy with what I have. Amen.

The Best Friend Ever

And I am convinced that nothing can ever separate us from his love. Whether we are high above the sky or in the deepest ocean, nothing in all creation will ever be able to separate us from the love of God that is revealed in Christ Jesus our Lord.

Romans 8:38-39 NLT

God loves you very much. And, hopefully, you love Him, too. The Bible tells us that nothing can keep us from the love of God. No matter where you go, or what happens to you, He loves you and He is always with you.

Do you feel lonely? Talk to Jesus . . . He is ready to listen! Are you feeling scared? He is right there with you. Jesus is the very best friend you could ever know. His love lasts forever. So, what are you waiting for? Let Him be your BFF—your best friend forever. Welcome Him into your heart right now.

THOUGHT OF THE DAY

God wrote the Bible because He has a lot of things He wants to tell you. Don't miss out!

PRAY TODAY

Dear God, today I just want to thank You for Your great love for me. Amen.

When Things Go Wrong

But as for you, be strong; don't be discouraged, for your work has a reward.

2 Chronicles 15:7 HCSB

Sometimes, there are days when everything seems to go wrong. You might wonder why nothing ever goes your way. But remember this: even when you're disappointed or hurt or upset with the way things turn out, God is near . . . and He loves you very much! And, while some things are hard to understand, God always has a plan!

If you're feeling disappointed, worried, sad, or afraid, you can talk to your parents and to God. You might just feel better about everything when you do!

THOUGHT OF THE DAY

Even on the very worst day, you can usually find some small thing to be thankful for. Give God thanks for that!

PRAY TODAY

Dear God, I know that You are always in control and I can trust You to take care of me. Thank You for loving me no matter what. Amen.

iF You PLay FaiR, You'Re a WinneR

Happiness comes to those who are fair to others and are always just and good.

Psalm 106:3 TLB

When you're playing games with other kids, God is watching . . . and He wants you to play fairly. Of course, everybody likes to win, so you may be tempted to do something that might give you an unfair advantage. But, that's a temptation you should resist.

People who cheat always get caught. Even if they think they've gotten away with something, God knows. And sooner or later, what you do will come back around to you. If you play fair . . . you are always a winner, even if you lose the game!

THOUGHT OF THE DAY

Winning is fun . . . but it takes courage to play fair!

PRAY TODAY

Dear God, help me to remember that You are always watching . . . and so are others. Help me to be fair and do what is right. Amen.

GOD IS BIGGER

I leave you peace; my peace I give you. I do not give it to you as the world does. So don't let your hearts be troubled or afraid.

John 14:27 NCV

The world can be a scary place sometimes. But when things happen that leave you feeling fearful, just remember that God is bigger than any problem you could have.

It's normal to feel afraid sometimes—but don't worry, God can take care of it! And don't forget to pray and ask God to give you His peace. Your parents can help you feel better too, so talk to them if you are scared. But no matter what happens, don't worry—God's got it covered!

THOUGHT OF THE DAY
Is there something that scares you? Talk to God about it!

PRAY TODAY
Dear God, whenever things get scary, help me remember that You are in charge of everything and I don't have to be afraid. Amen.

Don't Get Even . . . Forgive!

Repay no one evil for evil, but give thought to do what is honorable in the sight of all.

Romans 12:17 NCV

Have you read the story of Joseph in the Bible? He had some really bad things happen to him. He didn't do anything wrong, but he still ended up in jail and his own brothers sold him for money!

Do you think he was a little upset? Probably. But he forgave anyway, and God was able to turn everything around. He ended up running an entire country and saving his whole family from starving!

Has someone hurt you? Don't stay angry or try to get even. Instead, forgive them. God's way is always best!

THOUGHT OF THE DAY

Are you angry about something? Do you need to forgive someone? Don't wait . . . Do it now!

PRAY TODAY

Dear God, I don't think I have had as many problems as Joseph did. But I still get upset sometimes. Help me to forgive like he did. Amen.

What Love is

This is what real love is: It is not our love for God; it is God's love for us in sending his Son to be the way to take away our sins.

1 John 4:10 NCV

What is real love? God is always watching over you, always caring for you, always ready to hear you prayers, and always willing to forgive you, no matter what.

The Bible says that the very best thing God ever did to show us how much He loves us was sending His Son, Jesus, to die for us. So, today and every day, give God thanks for all of the love He has given you. Praise Him for His Son, for His blessings, for His protection, and for His life-giving love.

THOUGHT OF THE DAY

Love is patient, kind, and slow to get angry. Practice those three things today.

PRAY TODAY

Dear God, thank You for sending Your Son to this earth so that we could know what real love is. Amen.

everyone makes mistakes

"I will forgive their wrongdoings, and I will never again remember their sins," says the Lord.

Hebrews 8:12 NLT

Do you ever make mistakes? Of course you do! Everyone makes mistakes! When you do something wrong, here are some things you can do:

1. Say you are sorry and ask for forgiveness; 2. Fix the things you've messed up or broken, if you can; 3. Try not to make the same mistake again; 4. Ask God for His forgiveness (which, by the way, He always gives right away); 5. Forgive yourself–even if you made a really big mistake, you're still very, very special to God!

THOUGHT OF THE DAY

God forgives and forgets the moment you ask . . . so ask!

PRAY TODAY

Dear God, I know I make mistakes, and when I do, please help me be quick to ask for forgiveness. Amen.

Use Your Gifts

This is why I remind you to keep using the gift God gave you...

2 Timothy 1:6 NCV

You are unique! There has never been anyone just like you anywhere–ever. And one of the things that makes you special are the gifts God has given you.

What are you good at doing? Music or art? Sports or poetry? Maybe you are good at talking to people. Or maybe you are a great listener.

Whatever your special gifts are, practice and work hard at them. You never know what opportunities will come in the future and God wants you to use your gifts well!

THOUGHT OF THE DAY

It pays to practice. The more you practice, the better you'll become.

PRAY TODAY

Dear God, when I want to quit practicing and working hard, please help me keep going. I want to become what You made me to be. Amen.

Give Freely

Freely you have received; freely give.

Matthew 10:8 NIV

Lots of people in the world don't have all of the things you do. Some of these folks live in faraway places, and that can make it harder to help them. But there are some people who need your help who live very close by.

Ask your parents to help you find ways to do something nice for folks who need it. And don't forget that everybody needs love, kindness, and respect, so even if you don't have a lot of things to give, you can always share God's love with others. That's the very best gift of all!

THOUGHT OF THE DAY

Go through your room and closet and pick out 10 nice things you don't need or don't play with anymore and give them away.

PRAY TODAY

Dear God, thank You so much for the many gifts You have given me. Help me to always look for ways to show Your love. Amen.

a Friend That is True

A friend loves you all the time.

Proverbs 17:17 ICB

The Bible tells us that true friends love us all the time. How wonderful!

Bob and Larry know that "all the time" means a lot of things. It means when we do something wrong; when we are sad; when things go wrong; and even when wo mako oach other mad.

A true friend can make everything better, even in the worst of tlmes. Today, do something nice for a special friend. And don't forget to thank God for the friends He has given you!

THOUGHT OF THE DAY

A true friend is a gift of God.

PRAY TODAY

Dear God, thank You for my very best friend, Jesus. Help me love my friends the way Jesus loves me. Amen.

Be a Blessing

"It is more blessed to give than to receive."

Acts 20:35 ESV

Jesus said, "It is more blessed to give than to receive." That means that we shouldn't worry so much about what we have or don't have, and instead find ways to help others.

There are so many people—including some kids you know—who really need help. Ask your parents if there is something you can do to help a family who has less than you do. Or think of something simple and kind you can do for a teacher or neighbor. You'll be surprised by how wonderful it makes you feel!

THOUGHT OF THE DAY
Write your parents a note and let them know how much you appreciate them.

PRAY TODAY
Dear God, thank You for giving me everything I need. Help me share and give generously so I can be a blessing. Amen.

Right Here, Right Now

Fear not, for I am with you; Be not dismayed, for I am your God. I will strengthen you.

Isaiah 41:10 NKJV

Here's a promise you can depend on: Wherever you are, God is always there, too.

God doesn't take vacations, and He doesn't play hide-and-seek. He's always "right here, right now," ready to answer, ready to help, and waiting to hear from you. Whatever it is you need, God will take care of you. So don't be afraid.

If you have been wondering where God is, wonder no more. He's here. And that's a promise!

THOUGHT OF THE DAY

Can you think of three ways that you can tell God takes care of you?

PRAY TODAY

Dear God, I am glad that You are always with me and You are always listening to my thoughts and to my prayers. Amen.

He Cares For You

I will lift up my eyes to the hills–from whence comes my help? My help comes from the Lord, who made heaven and earth.

Psalm 121:1-2 NKJV

God cares about you. His love for you is amazing; it never changes–no matter what you do or don't do. Even when you make mistakes, God still loves you.

Sometimes, when you struggle, or fail, or do something wrong it is easy to think no one cares about you. You might feel like you don't even like yourself very much! But God thinks you are awesome. And He wants the very best for you today, tomorrow, and forever. So, whenever you are in trouble, call on God for help. He is ready to take care of you!

THOUGHT OF THE DAY

How is God's love similar to your parents'? Think about the ways they watch over you and take care of you. Make sure to tell them thank you!

PRAY TODAY

Dear God, because You love me, I don't need to worry about anything–I know You will protect me now and forever. Amen.

THE TRUTH CAN BE HARD

It is better to be poor and honest than to be foolish and tell lies.

Proverbs 19:1 ICB

Telling the truth can be hard sometimes. People might not always like what you have to say. If you're afraid to tell the truth, ask God for the courage to do the right thing, and then do it!

If you've ever told a big lie, and then had to live with the big consequences of that lie, you know that it's far more trouble to tell a lie than it is to tell the truth. So tell the truth, even when it's hard to do! You'll be glad you did.

THOUGHT OF THE DAY

Have you told your parents a lie? Even if it was a while ago, telling them the truth now is the right thing to do.

PRAY TODAY

Dear God, I want to be a person whose words are true and whose heart is pure. Help me always tell the truth. Amen.

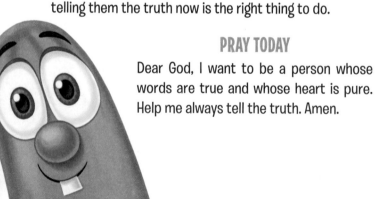

God Has a Plan

"I know what I am planning for you," says the Lord. "I have good plans for you, not plans to hurt you. I will give you hope and a good future."

Jeremiah 29:11 NCV

Did you know that God has a plan for your life? It's true! You can count on three things: 1. God loves you. 2. God wants what's best for you. 3. God has a plan for you.

God's plan may not always happen exactly like you want, but God always is working to give you a great future. Sometimes, even though you may want something very badly, you might need to be patient and wait. God's timing is always perfect.

Even if you don't get exactly what you want today, you can be sure that God wants what's best for you . . . always.

THOUGHT OF THE DAY

What do you want to be when you grow up? Why?

PRAY TODAY

Dear God, I don't always understand why things happen the way they do, but I know You have a plan and You will always take care of me. Amen.

Talk Less, Listen More

My dear brothers and sisters, always be willing to listen and slow to speak.

James 1:19 NCV

For most kids, talking is a lot more fun than listening. But it's easier to learn things with your eyes and ears, instead of your mouth. So, if you want to grow up healthy and smart, you should learn to listen carefully to the adults around you who have important lessons to teach.

When your parents, grandparents, or teachers are telling you something, do your best to pay attention. The more you listen to what they have to say, the more you'll learn.

THOUGHT OF THE DAY

Before you start talking, count to three and take a deep breath. Then ask yourself, is anyone else speaking?

PRAY TODAY

Dear God, sometimes it's really hard to stop and listen. Please help me open my ears and pay attention. Amen.

THE GOLDEN RULE

See that no one pays back evil for evil, but always try to do good to each other and to everyone else.

1 Thessalonians 5:15 TLB

Would you like to make the world a better place? If so, one of the best ways you can start is by practicing the Golden Rule.

Jesus said, "Whatever you want others to do for you, do also the same for them" (Matthew 7:12 HCSB). That means that you should treat other people the same way that you want to be treated. If you will do that, you might be surprised how people react. You can make a big difference wherever you go.

THOUGHT OF THE DAY

Think of two things you'd like for others to do for you, then do those things for your friends today!

PRAY TODAY

Dear God, help me always to do my very best to treat others the way I want to be treated. Amen.

a Great Day To Be Happy

This is the day that the Lord has made. Let us rejoice and be glad today!

Psalm 118:24 NCV

Every new day, including this one, is a wonderful treasure. Today is a priceless gift from God, and He wants you to think of it that way.

Whether you realize it or not, you have more things to be thankful for than you can count. But, it never hurts to try counting them anyway.

God has given you so much, so remember to thank Him today. Make an effort to find one or two things to be happy about today—no matter how small they are!

THOUGHT OF THE DAY

Each day is like a new, unopened present. You never know what you will find inside!

PRAY TODAY

Dear God, thank You for Your gift of today. It's so good to be happy! Amen.

Breaking Bad Habits

And you should follow my example, just as I follow Christ's.

1 Corinthians 11:1 TLB

Most people have a few habits they'd like to change, and maybe you do, too. If so, God can help. If you trust God, and if you keep asking Him to help you change your bad habits, He will help you.

The best way to change is to do your best to be like Jesus. If you follow His example, soon that habit won't be able to control you anymore. You can take control.

And don't worry if you slip up once in a while. If at first you don't succeed, keep trying and keep praying. God is listening, and He's ready to help you if you ask Him!

THOUGHT OF THE DAY

Do you have a bad habit you need to break? Ask your parents to help you come up with a plan. They will be glad to help!

PRAY TODAY

Dear God, today, I'm asking for Your help. Please help me change my bad habits into good ones, so what I do makes You happy. Amen.

a Pure Heart

Create in me a pure heart, God, and make my spirit right again.

Psalm 51:10 NCV

Other people see you from the outside. But God sees you from the inside–God sees your heart.

Everything about you–good or bad–comes out of your heart. The words you speak; your feelings and thoughts; the choices you make they all come from the heart.

If you ask God to give you a new, pure heart, He will. Then every good thing He puts inside you will shine on the outside, too. It is a beautiful thing!

THOUGHT OF THE DAY
Always remember–it's what's on the inside that counts.

PRAY TODAY
Dear God, please give me a new, clean and pure heart so I will think things and do things that are pleasing to You. Amen.

GOD IS PROUD OF YOU

"I am aware of all your good deeds–your kindness to the poor, your gifts and service to them; also I know your love and faith and patience, and I can see your constant improvement in all these things."

Revelation 2:19 TLB

You have been working hard to obey God and follow Him! But some days are harder than others. Sometimes, no matter how hard you try, you just can't get it right.

Do you sometimes feel like nobody notices that you are trying? Or do you get upset with yourself for not doing better? Don't worry! God's patience never ends and He sees all of your effort.

God is proud of you! And He won't give up on you . . . so don't quit!

THOUGHT OF THE DAY

Ask your parents how they think you are doing. You might be surprised!

PRAY TODAY

Dear God, sometimes I am not as patient or kind as I should be. Help me slow down and remember to do what You have taught me. Amen.

an Honest Heart

In every way be an example of doing good deeds. When you teach, do it with honesty and seriousness.

Titus 2:7 NCV

Where does honesty begin? In your own heart. If you sincerely want to be an honest person, then you should ask God to help you find the strength to be truthful all of the time.

That doesn't mean that you should always say everything that comes to your mind. Sometimes, the kind and loving thing to do is to just keep quiet. Especially if your words could hurt someone else's feelings.

But when it comes to a choice between the truth and a lie, make telling the truth such a habit that you don't even have to think about what to do.

THOUGHT OF THE DAY

What should you do if a friend asks you to lie for them?

PRAY TODAY

Dear God, please help me be truthful with You, with others, and also with myself. Amen.

YOUR VERY BEST FRIEND!

Then Jesus said, "I am the bread that gives life. Whoever comes to me will never be hungry, and whoever believes in me will never be thirsty."

John 6:35 NCV

Do you have a best friend? Someone who you love to hang out with and who likes the same stuff you do? Maybe you have a couple of great friends!

When you invite Jesus into your heart, you get a new best friend–forever. If you make mistakes, He'll still be your friend. If you behave badly, He'll still love you. If you feel sorry or sad, He can help you feel better.

Jesus is everything you will ever want or need. Hang out with Him today!

THOUGHT OF THE DAY

What are three things that a best friend should always do?

PRAY TODAY

Dear God, I am so glad that Jesus loves me and is my very best friend. Amen.

THE GIFT OF LAUGHTER

How we laughed and sang for joy. And the other nations said, "What amazing things the Lord has done for them."

Psalm 126:2 TLB

Do you like to laugh? Of course you do! Laughter is a gift from God that He hopes you'll use in the right way. So here are a few things to remember:

1. God wants you to be joyful. 2. Laughter is a great thing whon you're laughing at the right things. 3. You should laugh with people, but you should never laugh at them.

God created laughter for a reason . . . so laugh at the right things . . . and laugh a lot!

THOUGHT OF THE DAY

Nobody likes to laugh as much as the Peas. Philippe and Jean-Claude can get downright giggly. So if you are feeling a little down, just imagine them bouncing along!

PRAY TODAY

Dear God, help me to laugh and remember to share a happy smile with my family and friends every day. Amen.

CHOOSE TO BE JOYFUL!

"For the joy of the Lord is your strength. You must not be dejected and sad!"

Nehemiah 8:10 TLB

D o you know what joy is? Joy is not the same thing as happiness. Happiness is a feeling that is sometimes hard to find, depending on what is happening to us or around us.

But joy is not a feeling. It is a gift from God—one of the fruits of the Spirit—that helps us stay peaceful and content, no matter what is going on. It's how we know that God is in control, no matter what!

When bad stuff happens, the joy of the Lord is what makes you strong. Choose to be joyful today!

THOUGHT OF THE DAY

Joy does not depend on what's happening to you, but on God's love for you.

PRAY TODAY

Dear God, help me to always depend on Your joy. And help me to share it with others. Amen.

GOD'S BOOK

For I am not ashamed of the gospel, because it is God's power for salvation to everyone who believes.

Romans 1:16 HCSB

How do you get to know God? Well, one of the best ways is to read the book He wrote—the Bible.

You probably know that the Bible has lots of exciting stories. After all, Bob and Larry love to share their favorite Bibles stories—with a little Veggie twist. But there are also songs, letters, and lots of really smart advice. God wrote the Bible for you—so you would know what to do about any situation or problem. If you will read some of it every day, it will change your life!

THOUGHT OF THE DAY

Make a little time to read the Bible when you first get up—before you go to school or out to play. That way you won't forget!

PRAY TODAY

Dear God, the Bible has the answers to all of my questions and problems. Thank You for giving it to me. Amen.

STAND UP FOR WHAT'S RIGHT

We must obey God rather than men.

Acts 5:29 HCSB

Sometimes, we just go with the flow and do what our friends tell us to do. But going along with the crowd can be a dangerous thing.

It's not easy standing up to your friends when they want you to do something you know is wrong or foolish. You might wonder if they will like you anymore. Or worry that they will make fun of you.

There's no easy way around it—not giving in to peer pressure can be really hard. But doing something you know is wrong just to keep your friends isn't worth it. Don't be afraid to stand up for what is right!

THOUGHT OF THE DAY

Being obedient to God means that you cannot always please other people.

PRAY TODAY

Dear God, other people may want me to do things I know are wrong, but please help me do the right thing, even when it's hard. Amen.

Solomon Says . . . Be Kind!

A kind person is doing himself a favor. But a cruel person brings trouble upon himself.

Proverbs 11:17 ICB

King Solomon wrote most of the Book of Proverbs in the Bible and he gave us wonderful advice for living wisely. Solomon warned that unkind behavior only leads to trouble, but kindness is its own reward.

How does it make you feel when someone says something unkind to you? Is that what you would want to do to someone else?

The next time you're tempted to say an unkind word, remember the wisdom of Solomon and choose to be kind. You can be wise, too, by taking his advice to heart!

THOUGHT OF THE DAY

Be careful about what you say . . . words can hurt.

PRAY TODAY

Dear God, the Bible is full of wise advice about being kind, so it must be very important to You. Please help me to be kind. Amen.

FIBS GROW FAST!

Do not steal. Do not cheat one another. Do not lie.

Leviticus 19:11 NLT

Some people will tell you that telling a "little fib" is no big deal . . . after all, it's not really a lie. Well, don't believe it! A fib is a seed of dishonesty. And it will grow—fast!

When you tell a fib, or two, or three, before long you can't keep track of the truth anymore. Those fibs will keep on growing until they take over and you can't get out of the mess you have made.

A little lie is still a lie. And if you don't watch out, it will grow too big for you to handle!

THOUGHT OF THE DAY

It always pays to tell the truth, even when it's hard.

PRAY TODAY

Dear God, sometimes I don't always realize it when I tell little fibs. Please help me pay attention to my words and tell the truth. Amen.

Listen Carefully

Listen carefully to wisdom; set your mind on under-standing.

Proverbs 2:2 NCV

D o you listen carefully to the things your parents tell you? You should. Your parents want the very best for you. They want you to be happy and healthy; they want you to be smart and to do great things.

Your parents have a lot to teach you, and you have a lot to learn. So listen carefully to the things your mom and dad have to say. God loves us so much, and one of the ways he shows us that is by giving us parents.

THOUGHT OF THE DAY

Sometimes the smartest thing you can do is listen.

PRAY TODAY

Dear God, help me remember to listen respectfully to my parents, to my teachers, and to You. I know I have a lot to learn. Amen.

LIGHT OF THE WORLD

"You are the light of the world. A town built on a hill cannot be hidden. . . . Let your light shine before others, that they may see your good deeds and glorify your Father in heaven."

Matthew 5:14-16 NIV

Did you know that Jesus said you are the "light of the world"? That's a pretty big deal! When you think about how Jesus lived when He was here, it might seem impossible to live up to His example. But the good news is if He said it, then you can do it!

How can you be a light to the world? By sharing God's love, kindness, and joy with everyone you know. God made you to do amazing things and He gave you gifts that can make a big difference. So shine brightly . . . the world needs all the light it can get!

THOUGHT OF THE DAY

What can you do to let your light shine brighter at home and at school?

PRAY TODAY

Dear God, I want my light to shine brightly for You. Help me share love and kindness with everyone I meet. Amen.

Too Much Stuff

Don't be obsessed with getting more material things. Be relaxed with what you have.

Hebrews 13:5 MSG

How much stuff do you need to really be happy? Not as much as you might think. Because when it comes to the things we own, having too much is almost as bad having as too little.

There are kids all over the world who don't even have food, clothes, or shoes. There are some who live in your city! You already have so many good things, and if you aren't happy with what you have now, you probably won't be happy with more.

God doesn't want you to worry about stuff. It won't last long anyway!

THOUGHT OF THE DAY

Instead of thinking about what you want . . . figure out what you can give away.

PRAY TODAY

Dear God, I know that You have given me so many wonderful things. Help me be happy with what I have. Amen.

a Chance to Grow

For everyone has sinned; we all fall short of God's glorious standard.

Romans 3:23 NLT

Nobody likes mistakes, but everybody makes them. And you're no different! Mistakes are a part of growing up and a part of life.

When you make a mistake (and you will), just do your best to learn from it, and try not to do the same thing in the future.

The smart thing to do is to look at a mistake as a chance to grow. And if you do something that makes you feel a bit foolish, it couldn't hurt to laugh at yourself a little, too. Nobody is perfect!

THOUGHT OF THE DAY

What was your most embarrassing moment? Can you laugh about it?

PRAY TODAY

Dear God, the next time I make a mistake, help me to learn something, forgive myself, and maybe laugh a little, too. Amen.

never Be afraid to Do What's Right!

So don't worry, because I am with you. Don't be afraid, because I am your God.

Isaiah 41:10 NCV

The Bible tells us about Esther—a beautiful, regular, normal girl who became a queen. But that's not all she did—she became a hero, too.

God's people were in danger and Queen Esther was the only person who could help them. But going before the King uninvited was very dangerous—she could be thrown in jail, or worse! It took great courage to ask the King to save her people, but it was the right thing to do and she did it.

Don't ever be afraid to stand up for what you know is right because God is with you!

THOUGHT OF THE DAY

Doing the right thing can be scary some-times. But always remember that God is right there to help you do it!

PRAY TODAY

Dear God, thank You for giving me the courage to always stand up and do what is right. Amen.

The Shepherd

The Lord is my rock, my fortress, and my deliverer, my God, my mountain where I seek refuge. My shield, the horn of my salvation, my stronghold, my refuge, and my Savior.

2 Samuel 22:2-3 HCSB

Life isn't always easy. Far from it! Sometimes, life can really be very hard. But even when we're upset or hurt, we must remember that our Heavenly Father loves us.

When we're worried, God can reassure us; when we're sad, God can comfort us. When our feelings are hurt, God can make us feel better. Just like a shepherd takes care of his sheep, God takes care of you. He will protect you and keep you safe.

So if your day isn't going very well, go to God. He has everything you need.

THOUGHT OF THE DAY

Other than your parents, who do you go to when you have a problem or feel sad? Have you ever talked to God about it?

PRAY TODAY

Dear God, thank You for watching over me and protecting me. Amen.

Patience Takes Practice

Be gentle to all, able to teach, patient.

2 Timothy 2:24 NKJV

It is a good thing to be patient. But for most of us, it's a hard thing to do. After all, we have many things that we want, and we want them now! But the Bible tells us that we must learn to wait patiently for the things that God has for us.

Are you having trouble being patient? If so, remember that patience takes practice, and lots of it, so ask God to help you with that. And if you make a mistake, don't be too upset. After all, you should be patient with yourself, too.

THOUGHT OF THE DAY

What are some ways you can practice patience today?

PRAY TODAY

Dear God, sometimes it's very hard to be a patient person. Please help me do better, even when it's hard. Amen.

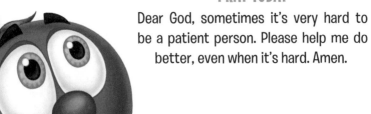

He Hears Every Prayer

Then if my people who are called by my name will humble themselves and pray and seek my face and turn from their wicked ways, I will hear from heaven and will forgive their sins and heal their land.

2 Chronicles 7:14 NLT

God promises that He hears your prayers–every one of them! So if you have a problem or something is bothering you, start praying. It's okay if you don't know exactly what to say. God understands even the things you can't put into words. Just spend time with Him.

Whatever you need, no matter how great or small, pray about it and never lose hope. God is not just near; He is right there with you, ready to talk and listen!

THOUGHT OF THE DAY
Ask your parents if you can spend some time each week praying together as a family.

PRAY TODAY
Dear God, thank You for hearing my prayers and for always being there for me. Amen.

Don't Be a Copy

Stay away from a foolish man; you will gain no knowledge from his speech.

Proverbs 14:7 HCSB

The truth is we all make mistakes–kids and grownups, too. But there is nothing worse than going along with someone else's bad choice, even though it seems like the easy thing to do.

The Bible tells us over and over that we should do the right thing, not the easy thing. Sometimes, we have to stand up for what we believe in, and that can be hard. But, God can help you do the right thing!

If your friends behave badly, don't copy them!

THOUGHT OF THE DAY
What is the smart thing to do? Choose wise friends!

PRAY TODAY
Dear God, help me do the right thing, even when others are doing the wrong thing. Amen.

You are Special

You're blessed when you're content with just who you are—no more, no less.

Matthew 5:5 MSG

When God made you, He gave you special talents and abilities that are yours and yours alone. That means you're a very special, one-of-a-kind person, with a one-of-a-kind life. But that doesn't mean that you should expect to be perfect. After all, only one person ever lived a perfect life, and that was Jesus.

It's okay to mess up and make mistakes. Jesus loves you just the way you are. Your parents feel the same way. And God wants you to love yourself, too.

THOUGHT OF THE DAY

Name three things that are special and wonderful about you!

PRAY TODAY

Dear God, I am thankful that You made me the way You did. Thank You for loving me just the way I am. Amen.

Don't Give Up!

Forgetting what is behind and straining toward what is ahead, I press on toward the goal to win the prize for which God has called me heavenward in Christ Jesus.

Philippians 3:13-14 NIV

At one time or another, we all are tempted to give up. Why? Perhaps we are afraid that we might be embarrassed if we try hard but don't succeed. Maybe we think we can't do it, so there is no point in trying. Maybe we've given it all we've got, but it's just so very difficult we don't think we can go on.

God can do amazing things when we depend on Him to help us keep trying. But if you quit at the first sign of trouble, you'll never find out what God can do through you. So don't give up!

THOUGHT OF THE DAY

If you don't try, nothing will happen. When you do—anything is possible!

PRAY TODAY

Dear God, when I am tempted to give up, help me to keep going and not quit. Amen.

LOOK FOR GOD

Continue to ask, and God will give to you. Continue to search, and you will find. Continue to knock, and the door will open for you.

Matthew 7:7 ICB

The Bible tells us that if we want to know God, we should look for Him. But how do we do that? By reading the Bible. By going to church. And most definitely by praying, which really just means talking to Him.

Sometimes, of course, when we're tired, angry, or frustrated, it is very hard for us to feel like talking to God. Thankfully, anger and frustration are feelings that come and go, but God's love lasts forever.

If you are willing to look for God, He is ready to be found. He is always waiting to talk to you. He's listening now!

THOUGHT OF THE DAY

Do you sometimes bug your parents by asking too many questions? Good news: God loves questions! Ask Him everything!

PRAY TODAY

Dear God, I want to know everything about You. Help me never give up looking for You so I can find You. Amen.

aLL THe Time

The LORD is my strength and song, and He has become my salvation; He is my God, and I will praise Him.

Exodus 15:2 NIV

When is the best time to praise God? In church on Sunday? Before dinner is served? At bedtime? Those are all good, but the very best time to praise God is all day, every day, as much as you can!

When we know God and love God, He puts a happy song in our hearts. You just can't help but tell God how great He is and how much you love Him!

So, every day, all the time, talk to God about what's bothering you and praise Him for all the good things He has done. God always hears and always answers!

THOUGHT OF THE DAY

Praise God every day!

PRAY TODAY

Dear God, I want to praise You all the time. Thank You for loving me and always listening. Amen.

THE BIG PICTURE

I said to myself, "Relax and rest. God has showered you with blessings."

Psalm 116:7 MSG

Remembering all the great things God has done for you can change how you look at the not-so-good things that can happen sometimes. It's what we call "perspective"—a big word that really means looking at the "big picture."

Here are a few things to think about today:

#1 God made you and loves you forever.
#2 God sent His Son, Jesus, to give you eternal life.
#3 God has a great plan for your life.
#4 God has given you talents and abilities so you can grow and do amazing things.

THOUGHT OF THE DAY

If you remember God's blessings and keep your eyes on the big picture, it is easy to relax and trust God.

PRAY TODAY

Dear God, thank You for all the blessings You have given me. I'm going to relax and trust You today. Amen.

Practice, Practice, Practice

All athletes practice strict self-control. They do it to win a prize that will fade away, but we do it for an eternal prize.

1 Corinthians 9:25 NLT

The Book of Proverbs tells us that self-control and patience are very good things to have. But for most of us, self-control and patience can also be very hard things to learn.

Are you having trouble being patient? And are you having trouble slowing down long enough to think before you act? If so, remember that self-control takes practice, and lots of it, so keep trying. And if you make a mistake, it's okay. Just try again and ask God for help to do better.

THOUGHT OF THE DAY
You are what you eat; and you do what you think!

PRAY TODAY
Dear God, thank You for helping me control myself and be patient so I can succeed. Amen.

You've Got Talent!

God has given gifts to each of you from his great variety of spiritual gifts. Manage them well so that God's generosity can flow through you.

1 Peter 4:10 NLT

There's nobody exactly like you. God has given you a special combination of talents, and He has given you one-of-a-kind opportunities to share those talents with the world.

There's an old saying: "What you are is God's gift to you; what you become is your gift to God." Today, do your best to use your talents to help your family, your friends, and the world around you—starting with your neighborhood, school, and church. There is no limit to what God can do through you!

THOUGHT OF THE DAY

Just because you have talent doesn't mean you don't have to practice. Practice makes perfect!

PRAY TODAY

Dear God, thank You for giving me talents and gifts. Help me to use them to help other people. Amen.

You Can Always Trust God

Commit everything you do to the Lord. Trust him, and he will help you.

Psalm 37:5 NLT

Sometimes, people will let you down, but God never will. You can always trust God because He will never leave you, not even for a moment, and He will never tell you a lie.

The Bible makes many promises, and God always keeps every single one of them. He never breaks His Word and He is always there to help you. So remember this: No matter where you are or what you're going, the Lord is with you, and He's on your side. Always!

THOUGHT OF THE DAY

Even when you don't understand what He's doing, you can be sure that He loves you very much!

PRAY TODAY

Dear God, thank You for always loving me and always keeping Your promises to me. Amen.

Wisdom is as Wisdom Does

Are there those among you who are truly wise and understanding? Then they should show it by living right and doing good things with a gentleness that comes from wisdom.

James 3:13 NCV

If you'd like to learn to make good and wise decisions, there are many ways you can do it. You can start by listening carefully to your parents, your grandparents, and your teachers. You can read lots of books, and you can spend lots of time reading the most important book of all: the Bible.

Would you like to grow up to be a very wise person? Then keep listening and learning. Study God's Word. And then, put that wisdom into action, by living it!

THOUGHT OF THE DAY

Being smart at school isn't always the same thing as being wise.

PRAY TODAY

Dear God, I want to become wiser and learn to make good choices. Thank You for helping me. Amen.

KIND THOUGHTS

A wise person is patient. He will be honored if he ignores a wrong done against him.

Proverbs 19:11 ICB

What does it mean to forgive? Forgiveness means that you decide not to stay mad at somebody who has done something wrong. You change your angry thoughts to kind thoughts.

Forgiveness usually happens when you decide that making God happy is more important than staying angry. Forgiving also can help you feel better, too, because being angry usually hurts you more than anyone else.

Sometimes forgiveness can be very hard if our feelings have really been hurt, but it's worth the effort!

THOUGHT OF THE DAY

Are you mad at someone? Think of two nice things you can say the next time you see them.

PRAY TODAY

Dear God, whenever I am angry, please give me a forgiving heart. And help me remember to think kind thoughts. Amen.

Be a Good Friend

Be kind to each other, tenderhearted, forgiving one another, just as God through Christ has forgiven you.

Ephesians 4:32 NLT

The best way to have a good friend is to be a good friend. Think about what you like about your friends. Do they tell you the truth? Are they always on your side? Do they forgive you when you mess up?

If those things are important to you, then it is wise to remember to treat others the same way. When you do, you'll soon discover that most people will be nice to you, too. And when you're kind to everybody, you share the love of Jesus, your best friend of all!

THOUGHT OF THE DAY

Jimmy and Jerry have been friends for a really long time. Why? Because they always try to be kind and forgiving.

PRAY TODAY

Dear God, thank You for the friends You have given me. Help me to always be a good friend. Amen.

a Life of Godliness

Knowing God leads to self-control. Self-control leads to patient endurance, and patient endurance leads to godliness.

2 Peter 1:6 NLT

Your relationship with God will last for the rest of your life. As you grow and spend more time with God, you become the person He wants you to be.

First, God helps you learn self-control, which then leads to patience. Finally, as you get better and better at controlling yourself and patiently waiting on God, you begin to live a life of godliness—in other words, you will look, talk, and act like your Heavenly Father. What could be better?

THOUGHT OF THE DAY

Staying in control or waiting patiently is not easy. But with God's help, you can do it!

PRAY TODAY

Dear God, sometimes I am not very patient. Help me slow down and be still. I want to be like You. Amen.

God's Power

I pray . . . that you may know . . . his uncomparably great power for us who believe.

Ephesians 1:18-19 NIV

How strong is God? Stronger than anybody can imagine! But even if we can't totally understand God's power, we can be sure that God will guide and protect us forever.

The next time you're worried or afraid, remember this: if God is powerful enough to create the universe and everything in it, He's also strong enough to take care of you. Nothing is too big for Him to handle. Now that's a comforting thought!

THOUGHT OF THE DAY

There is nothing you can't face when God is at your side!

PRAY TODAY

Thank You, God, that I can trust You for everything in my life. And thank You that when I feel afraid You are there at my side loving and taking care of me. Amen.

STOP AND THINK

Now you must rid yourselves of all such things as these: anger, rage, malice. . . .

Colossians 3:8 NIV

When we get upset or angry, sometimes we say or do things that hurt others or ourselves. The Bible tells us that it is foolish to become too angry too quickly and that it is wise to remain calm. That's why we should learn to slow down and think about things before we do them.

Do you want to make life better for yourself and for your family? Then when something goes wrong or someone does something that upsets you, stop and think before you say or do something, not after. It's the wise thing to do.

THOUGHT OF THE DAY

If you're a little angry, think carefully before you speak. If you're very angry, think very carefully!

PRAY TODAY

Dear God, help me calm down when I get upset or angry and think things through. Amen.

Jesus Loves You!

You're blessed when you're content with just who you are—no more, no less.

Matthew 5:5 MSG

Have you heard the song "Jesus Loves Me"? Probably so. It's a simple song that should remind you of this important fact: Jesus loves you very much.

When you invite Jesus into your heart, He'll love and protect you forever. If you have problems, He'll help you solve them. Even when you make mistakes or do something wrong, He still loves you. If you feel sorry or sad, He can help you feel better.

Jesus loves you. Simple, but so true. And that is awesome!

THOUGHT OF THE DAY

God made you special, and He loves you very much!

PRAY TODAY

Dear God, loving You is the best decision I could ever make. Thank You for filling my heart with strength, hope, and love. Amen.

The Blame Game

People's own foolishness ruins their lives, but in their minds they blame the Lord.

Proverbs 19:3 NCV

When something goes wrong, do you look for somebody to blame? Do you try to get other people in trouble, even if you're the one who made the mistake?

Nobody likes to admit they have messed up. It can be really hard to admit when you are wrong, even if you just accidently make a mistake.

If you've made a mistake or done something wrong, don't try to blame somebody else. Look for a way to say, "I'm sorry, and I won't make that same mistake again."

THOUGHT OF THE DAY

When you make a mistake, be honest and accept the consequences.

PRAY TODAY

Dear God, when I make a mistake, help me accept responsibility and learn from it. Amen.

ALWAYS DO WHAT'S RIGHT

So don't get tired of doing what is good. Don't get discouraged and give up, for we will reap a harvest of blessing at the appropriate time.

Galatians 6:9 NLT

It can seem like fun sometimes to do things you know aren't "good," especially if your friends want to. But doing the right thing always works out for the best—for you and for everyone.

It's always the right time to make good choices. Even when your parents and teachers aren't watching, God is. He knows how hard it can be to make the right choice. But eventually, your good choices will be rewarded. It's always the right time to do what is right!

THOUGHT OF THE DAY

Sometimes it is hard to say "no." Ask your parents for an idea of what to say when you need to make the right choice.

PRAY TODAY

Dear God, it is really hard sometimes to do the right thing. Thank You for helping me make the right choices. Amen.

a Transformation

But endurance must do its complete work, so that you may be mature and complete, lacking nothing.

James 1:4 HCSB

Do you know how a butterfly is born? While a caterpillar rests inside its cocoon, many changes happen, including the development of wings. But when the butterfly's body is finally finished changing, he still has to struggle to break out, or his wings will never be strong enough to fly.

By trying and trying—and seemingly failing and failing—the butterfly is transformed and comes out ready to do what it was created for. The same is true for you!

THOUGHT OF THE DAY

Do you have a hobby or special skill you are good at? How does practicing help you get better?

PRAY TODAY

Dear God, help me not get discouraged when things don't go the way I think they should. I want to stick with it and never give up. Amen.

Keep Burning!

Don't burn out; keep yourselves fueled and aflame. Be alert servants of the Master, cheerfully expectant. Don't quit in hard times; pray all the harder.

Romans 12:11-12 MSG

Like most kids, you are probably super busy. Friends, family time, church, and maybe school or sports activities all keep you going from morning to night! But here's a question: do you make time in your schedule for God? Hopefully so!

If you'll take the time every day to pray and thank God for your blessings, the rest will fall into place. Instead of burning out, He will help you keep your fire going!

Nothing is as important as spending time with your Heavenly Father.

THOUGHT OF THE DAY

Sometimes too much is just too much. Talk to your parents about your activities and see if there is something you would rather not do.

PRAY TODAY

Dear God, I have lots of things to do, but nothing is more important than You. Help me make time for You every day. Amen.

SERVE THE LORD

Do not be lazy but work hard, serving the Lord with all your heart.

Romans 12:11 NCV

The Bible says it over and over again: It's important to serve other people. Serving can mean many different things. You can help your mom clean the house. You could help a friend with their homework. You could partioipate in a fund raiser for a special cause. You could write a letter to someone in your family that you don't see very often. Whatever God leads you to do, work hard and He will bless you!

THOUGHT OF THE DAY

It sounds strange, but it's true: the more you serve others, the better it makes you feel.

PRAY TODAY

Dear God, I want to do what I can to serve others. Please show me what You want me to do and I will do it with all my heart. Amen.

You Can Do It!

"Be strong and courageous and do it. Do not be afraid and do not be dismayed, for the Lord God, even my God, is with you. He will not leave you or forsake you."

1 Chronicles 28:20 ESV

Do you ever get scared when you have a big problem? We all feel that way sometimes.

David had to face fear when he defeated Goliath. But he stepped up and beat that giant anyway. How was he able to do that? Because David knew God was with him and would take care of him—no matter what. So he chose to be strong and courageous . . . and do it!

If you're too afraid to try, you'll never find out what great things you and God can do. So go for it!

THOUGHT OF THE DAY

David wasn't afraid to try something hard. Just do your best and don't give up.

PRAY TODAY

Dear God, thank You that You are always with me and that I don't have to be afraid. Amen.

a Home Filled with Love

But Ruth said, "Don't beg me to leave you or to stop following you. Where you go, I will go. Where you live, I will live. Your people will be my people, and your God will be my God."

Ruth 1:16 NCV

What makes a family? Love.

The Bible tells the story of Ruth, a special girl who really knew how to love her family. Ruth's husband died, but she chose to stay with her mother-in-law and take care of her, no matter what.

Ruth worked hard and God rewarded her for her faithfulness. He gave Ruth a new husband and children, and one of Ruth's descendants was Jesus.

Love your family the way that Ruth loved hers, and you will be blessed!

THOUGHT OF THE DAY

What are three things you can do to help your home stay filled with love?

PRAY TODAY

Dear God, help me remember that next to You, my family should always come first. Thank You for blessing us. Amen.

Slow Down!

Knowing God leads to self-control. Self-control leads to patient endurance, and patient endurance leads to godliness.

2 Peter 1:6 NLT

Are you one of those kids who tries to do everything fast, faster, or fastest? Do you sometimes do things before you stop to think about the consequences of your actions?

If that's the case, it's probably a good idea to start learning to think about things before you act. And think before you speak, too. When you do, you'll learn that you can avoid lots of problems and trouble!

God doesn't want to take away all your fun. He wants to give you self-control so you can become the person He wants you to be.

THOUGHT OF THE DAY

One of the wisest things you can do is just think before you do something.

PRAY TODAY

Dear God, please help me slow down a little and think about things before I do them. Amen.

CHOOSE JOY

Always be full of joy in the Lord. I say it again–rejoice!

Philippians 4:4 NLT

Do you know why God tells us to "be full of joy"? Because joy can make every day a great day, even when things aren't going just right.

All of us have bad feelings sometimes, but without joy, bad feelings can take over and make us too weak to do anything! With joy, almost anything is possible!

Joy brings confidence in God. It give us hope in times of trouble. It makes every good thing in our lives so much better. Choose to be full of joy today!

THOUGHT OF THE DAY

If something scares you, like a trip to the dentist, choose to make it joyful! Wear a silly costume or hat and look for every chance to laugh and have fun!

PRAY TODAY

Dear God, I will choose to be joyful, so I don't miss out on all the wonderful things You have for me. Amen.

GOD IS LOOKING AFTER YOU!

The Lord is my light and my salvation; whom shall I fear? The Lord is the strength of my life; of whom shall I be afraid?

Psalm 27:1 NKJV

Sometimes you may feel afraid. Everyone does. It's pretty normal. But the Bible tells us that with God we don't have to be afraid. He's bigger and stronger than anything that might make you scared!

Thankfully, God never leaves you, not even for a moment. He's always there to protect you.

God keeps His promises, and He wants you to trust Him completely. When you do, you don't have to be afraid.

THOUGHT OF THE DAY

Be brave! You and God together can handle anything!

PRAY TODAY

Dear God, thank You for always watching out for me and keeping me safe. Thank You for keeping my family safe too. Amen.

a GReaT LiFe

I came so they can have real and eternal life, more and better life than they ever dreamed of.

John 10:10 MSG

God has big plans for you; plans for many good things and for a great life! He wants you to be happy and have fun. He wants you to love your family and be kind to your friends. He wants you to do something special with your life that only you can do. His blessings just keep on coming.

So remember this: Your life is an amazing opportunity. Do your best to make good choices and obey God. When you do, good things will happen . . . lots of good things!

THOUGHT OF THE DAY
God has a purpose for everything—including you!

PRAY TODAY
Dear God, thank You for everything You have done for me. I am excited about the great plans You have for my life! Amen.

FORGIVE AND FORGET

And forgive our sins—for we have forgiven those who sinned against us.

Luke 11:4 TLB

Have you heard the saying, "Forgive and forget"? Well, it might sound simple, but it's not. It can be hard enough to forgive sometimes, but then to forget what happened, too? Incredible!

The Bible says that God forgets our mistakes when we ask for forgiveness. How cool is that? Wouldn't it be great if you could really forgive and forget the next time your friend does something that hurts your feelings? Imagine how much better your friendship could be!

THOUGHT OF THE DAY

Isn't it amazing that God completely forgives and forgets our mistakes?

PRAY TODAY

Dear God, when somebody hurts my feelings, help me forgive them so well that I can't remember what they did! Amen.

a Promise of Love

His banner over me was love.

Song of Solomon 2:4 KJV

God makes lots of amazing promises in the Bible, but the biggest one of all is that He loves you. No matter what. Forever. And it's a promise that He will keep.

No matter where you are (and no matter what you have done), you can never lose God's love. It might be hard to understand that with your head, so just believe Him and receive His love with your heart.

You are God's special child. His love will always be there for you. No matter what!

THOUGHT OF THE DAY

God shows His love for you in a million ways, big and small. Can you think of three you noticed today?

PRAY TODAY

Dear God, the Bible teaches me that You are my loving Father. Thank You for loving me so much. Amen.

Two Sisters

"Lord, don't you care that my sister has left me to do the work by myself? Tell her to help me!"

Luke 10:40 NIV

Do you have a brother or sister that you have a hard time getting along with sometimes? The Bible tells us the story of two sisters who weren't exactly seeing eye-to-eye.

Jesus came to visit and Martha was worried about getting stuff done. Her sister Mary just wanted to sit and spend time with Jesus.

Jesus said that Mary made the better choice. Why? Because in that situation, even though getting the work done was good, spending time with Jesus was the most important thing.

THOUGHT OF THE DAY

What could Mary and Martha have done differently to get along better?

PRAY TODAY

Dear God, please help me to not get so busy with stuff in my life that I forget to spend time with You. Amen.

The Way to Live

Good people will be guided by honesty; dishonesty will destroy those who are not trustworthy.

Proverbs 11:3 NCV

How do you feel when somebody tells you something that isn't true? You probably feel mad, or sad, or bad, or all three!

Even little lies have a way of growing fast. And the big ones can really hurt others and make really big messes.

If you want other people to tell you the truth, you should always be truthful with them. Honesty isn't just the best policy; it's also the way God wants you to live. So do your best to tell the truth, even when it's hard.

THOUGHT OF THE DAY

Telling lies is like getting caught in a bear trap. There's no easy way out!

PRAY TODAY

Dear God, I don't like it when people lie to me, so please help me always be truthful. Amen.

Kindness and Respect

Just as you want others to do for you, do the same for them.

Luke 6:31 HCSB

How do you think God wants you to treat people? It's simple really–He wants you to treat others exactly the way you want to be treated: with kindness, respect, and good manners.

Respect makes a big difference, because it means treating people like they matter. And they do! They are very important to God!

Kindness is also important, because it shows people how much God loves them.

Always remember to show respect and kindness and use your best manners. You would want others to do the same for you!

THOUGHT OF THE DAY

Before you say or do something you shouldn't, think about how it will make the other person feel.

PRAY TODAY

Dear God, I want to be respectful and kind to others. Help me always to do my very best to treat others the way I want to be treated. Amen.

JUST BELIEVE!

Don't be afraid. Only believe.

Mark 5:36 HCSB

Do you remember the story of Daniel in the Lion's Den? Daniel, who loved and obeyed God, was thrown in a hole to be lunch for the hungry lions! But God protected him and everything turned out better than it was before!

Hopefully, you'll never be in a situation quite like that. But is there something that has you scared or afraid you will fail? God says, don't be afraid! Just believe Him and do your best. He'll take care of the rest!

THOUGHT OF THE DAY

You can't be too afraid to try if you want to do great things!

PRAY TODAY

Dear God, thank You for taking care of me so I don't have to be afraid. I choose to believe You! Amen.

Growing in Grace

But grow in the grace and knowledge of our Lord and Savior Jesus Christ. To Him be the glory both now and forever. Amen.

2 Peter 3:18 NKJV

What does it mean to "grow in grace and knowledge"? First, knowledge is how much you know about something. You can learn more about God by reading the Bible, talking with your parents, and going to Sunday School and church.

Growing in grace begins to happen when we start to relax and trust God to take care of everything we need—just because He loves us. You can't earn God's love and grace; they are His free gifts to you!

Today, think about how you can learn something new about God, and trust Him more, too.

THOUGHT OF THE DAY

To learn more about God, read your Bible every day.

PRAY TODAY

Dear God, thank You for loving me just because You do. Help me grow in knowledge and grace so I can know You better! Amen.

WHAT IS PATIENCE?

Therefore, God's chosen ones, holy and loved, put on heartfelt compassion, kindness, humility, gentleness, and patience.

Colossians 3:12 HCSB

The dictionary defines the word *patience* as "the ability to be calm, tolerant, and understanding."

Here's what that means: "calm" means being in control of your emotions (not letting your emotions control you). "Tolerant" means being kind and considerate to people who are different from you. And "understanding" means being able to put yourself in another person's shoes.

That's exactly the kind of person that God wants you to be.

THOUGHT OF THE DAY

The best things in life rarely happen suddenly . . . they usually take time.

PRAY TODAY

Dear God, please help me become calm, tolerant, and understanding so I can become the person You want me to be. Amen.

Live in Peace

It is good and pleasant when God's people live together in peace!

Psalm 133:1 NCV

What kind of friend are you? Are you kind, thoughtful, and peaceful? Hopefully, that's how you are and your friends treat you that way too.

The Bible says it is good and pleasant when God's people live together in peace. Whether you are at school, church, or home, how you get along with others will make your life either great . . . or not.

Living in peace takes some work, but it makes everyone so much happier. So do your best to share God's love wherever you are and peace will follow.

THOUGHT OF THE DAY

Junior always likes to start his day with a big "Good morning!" What can you do to make someone's day better?

PRAY TODAY

Dear God, thank You for my friends. Help me to always put love and peace first. Amen.

Talk it Out

Those who are sad now are happy, because God will comfort them.

Matthew 5:4 NCV

Whenever you are feeling sad, talk to your parents and to God about your feelings.

Talking with your parents is helpful because they understand that the problems that seem very big to you today probably won't seem so big tomorrow.

Talking with God helps because God knows exactly how you feel and He helps make things better.

So the next time you're sad, don't hold your feelings inside. You'll be glad you asked for help.

THOUGHT OF THE DAY

Get a journal and start writing down your questions and feelings. You'll be surprised how much it helps!

PRAY TODAY

Dear God, when I am sad, I know that I can talk to my parents . . . and to You. Thank You for listening to me and comforting me. Amen.

Good Manners Matter

Let everyone see that you are considerate in all you do.

Philippians 4:5 NLT

Do you like it when people use good manners? Of course you do! And, since the Golden Rule says that you should treat other people like you want to be treated, you should always be kind and use good manners, too.

Being polite isn't very hard. Simple things like saying "please," "thank you," and "excuse me" or letting someone else go first can go a long way.

Lots of good things happen when you show respect for all people. You might even make some new friends!

THOUGHT OF THE DAY

Do your best today to remember to always say "Please" and "Thank you."

PRAY TODAY

Dear God, I know good manners matter to You. Please help me to remember them and use them every day. Amen.

When You Look in the Mirror

Do you not know that you are the temple of God and that the Spirit of God dwells in you?

1 Corinthians 3:16 NKJV

D o you like the person you see when you look in the mirror? You should! After all, you are a very special person who is made—and loved—by God.

The Bible says that God made you in His image, and when you ask Jesus into your heart, the Spirit of God comes to live inside you! That means you look like Him on the outside and on the inside!

So the next time you look in the mirror, don't be hard on yourself. Look at yourself the way God sees you and say out loud: "I am special and wonderful!"

THOUGHT OF THE DAY

You matter—not because of what you can do, but simply because God made you.

PRAY TODAY

Dear God, thank You for making me and loving me. Because You love me, I will feel good about myself. Amen.

You Can Always Trust God

Those who trust in the Lord are as secure as Mount Zion; they will not be defeated but will endure forever.

Psalm 125:1 NLT

Do you know the story of Gideon? He was a mighty warrior in the Bible—who didn't think he was very mighty at all. But he trusted and obeyed God.

God told Gideon that He would defeat a huge army with just 300 men. And they did. What did they fight with? Each man had a trumpet, an empty pitcher, and a lamp. Sounds crazy, doesn't it? Crazy—but true.

God had a plan and Gideon followed His directions. The rest was easy. No matter how crazy or impossible it sounds, you can always trust God!

THOUGHT OF THE DAY

Can you think of something crazy—but true—that God has done for you?

PRAY TODAY

Dear God, sometimes I feel a lot like Gideon. That I can't really do what You have asked me to do. But I will trust and obey You, too. Amen.

Make Some Lemonade

Every day is hard for those who suffer, but a happy heart is like a continual feast.

Proverbs 15:15 NCV

Have you read the story of Joseph in the Bible? Lots of bad things happened to him. He could have been angry and mean, and felt really sorry for himself. But he didn't.

Instead, every time something bad happened, Joseph just worked harder. He stayed cheerful, trusted God, and had a great attitude.

There's a famous saying that says, "When life hands you lemons, make lemonade." When bad things happen, you can get angry, whine, and complain. Or you can make the best of a bad situation and make some lemonade, just like Joseph.

THOUGHT OF THE DAY

In a bad situation, look for something to be thankful for!

PRAY TODAY

Dear God, I know bad things happen sometimes. When they do, help me have a good attitude and find something good I can do. Amen.

ask for Help

And no temptation is irresistible. You can trust God to keep the temptation from becoming so strong that you can't stand up against it, for he has promised this and will do what he says. He will show you how to escape temptation's power . . .

1 Corinthians 10:13 TLB

Everybody faces "temptation"–which is when you want to do something you know you shouldn't do. It can happen anytime, anywhere–sometimes when you least expect it!

The best way to fight temptation is to ask for help. Why? Because sometimes temptation is just too strong to resist by yourself.

Whether it's video games, or chocolate, or watching too much TV–the next time you are tempted ask your friends, family, and God for help!

THOUGHT OF THE DAY

What things are the biggest temptations for you?

PRAY TODAY

Dear God, thank You for helping me stay strong and resist temptation. Help me remember to ask for help when I am tempted. Amen.

The importance of Family

"And I will be a father to you, and you shall be sons and daughters to me, says the Lord Almighty."

2 Corinthians 6:18 ESV

Your family is a wonderful, one-of-a-kind gift from God. What a blessing it is to be loved!

Have you ever really stopped to think about how important family is? Your parents love you, of course, and so does everybody else in your family. But it doesn't stop there. You're also an important part of God's family and He loves you more than you can imagine.

What if you or someone you know doesn't have a family who loves them? That's when we have to step in and be their family–the family of God!

THOUGHT OF THE DAY

What makes your family unique and special?

PRAY TODAY

Dear God, help me show my family–and Your family–that I love them by the things that I say and do. Amen.

JUST STAY CALM

A patient person [shows] great understanding, but a quick-tempered one promotes foolishness.

Proverbs 14:29 HCSB

Temper tantrums are so silly. And so is pouting and whining. Nobody likes it when things don't go their way, but when we lose our tempers, we can say things that we shouldn't say, and we can do things that we shouldn't do.

The Bible tells us that it is foolish to become angry and that it is wise to remain calm. That's why we should ask God to help us control our tempers before our tempers control us. If you start to feel mad, take a deep breath and pray. God will always be there to help!

THOUGHT OF THE DAY

When you get mad, it's better to think before saying anything. Once you say it, you can't "un-say" it!

PRAY TODAY

Dear God, help me to remember to turn to You when something happens that makes me angry. Amen.

FOR SUCH A TIME AS THIS

"Who knows? Maybe you were made queen for just such a time as this."

Esther 4:14 MSG

The story of Esther is a wonderful example of how one person can make a big difference if they trust God. Esther risked her life to save her people when no one else could save them, and even today the Jewish people still celebrate the holiday of Purim to remember her courage.

Esther was destined for greatness . . . she just didn't know it. You are destined for greatness too . . . even if you don't realize it. So do your best to have courage and trust God's plan. Great things are going to happen!

THOUGHT OF THE DAY

It is no accident that you are alive right here and right now. You were born for such a time as this!

PRAY TODAY

Dear God, with Your help I know I can do great things too. Thank You for making a special plan just for me! Amen.

Make God Proud

And a voice from heaven said, "You are my dearly loved Son, and you bring me great joy."

Mark 1:11 NLT

D id you know that Jesus made his Heavenly Father proud? The Bible says God was pleased to watch Jesus grow in wisdom, strength, and favor. God loves His Son just like your parents love you and are proud to watch you grow.

The Bible tells us that when we trust in Jesus as our Savior, we become children of God. He loves to see all His children giving love and kindness, working hard, and learning about Him. He's proud of you too!

THOUGHT OF THE DAY

What are three things you can do today that would make God proud?

PRAY TODAY

Dear God, please help me to be more like Jesus. I want to make You proud, too. Amen.

GOOD AND EVIL

Hold on to what is good. Stay away from every kind of evil.

1 Thessalonians 5:21-22 HCSB

Let's face it–a lot of bad things happen in the world. Some things happen that aren't anyone's fault, like sickness or terrible storms. But other things, like bullying, stealing, or lying, are no accident–and they can have big consequences!

What is a kid to do? You can't fix everything. But you can stand up for what you know is right. Just ask Him and God will help you hold on to what is good!

THOUGHT OF THE DAY

Do you ever feel sad or worried about things that happen? Talk to your Mom and Dad. They can help you come up with ideas to help.

PRAY TODAY

Dear God, when other people do bad things, help me to do what is right and good. Amen.

God's Treasure Map

Every part of Scripture is God-breathed and useful one way or another.

2 Timothy 3:16 MSG

Do you think about the Bible a lot? Hopefully, you make time to read the Bible and learn about God every day. After all, the Bible is God's message to you. It's not just a book, it's a priceless treasure map, full of wonderful secrets waiting to be discovered.

No matter what questions or problems you might have, the Bible always is the best place to go for answers. So go ahead and start reading your Bible now—you never know what treasure you might find!

THOUGHT OF THE DAY

Ask your parents if you can have a weekly family time where you read from the Bible together and talk about what you learn.

PRAY TODAY

Dear God, the Bible is Your gift to me. Help me to use it, trust it, and follow it every day. Amen.

a Wonderful Place

Be glad and rejoice, because your reward is great in heaven.

Matthew 5:12 HCSB

The Bible makes this important promise: when you give your heart to Jesus, you will live forever with Him in heaven. Have you ever wondered what heaven is like? The Bible tells us a little, but most of what heaven will be like is a mystery.

Even though we don't know everything about heaven, we do know that heaven is a wonderful place; a place of joy and wonder; a place where we will be reunited with our loved ones and with God. It's wonderful to think about . . . and it's waiting for you!

THOUGHT OF THE DAY

You can trust that heaven will be amazing because God is amazing!

PRAY TODAY

Dear God, I can't wait to see everything You have prepared for me in heaven! Amen.

Practice Forgiveness

"Lord, how often will my brother sin against me, and I forgive him? As many as seven times?" Jesus said to him, "I do not say to you seven times, but seventy-seven times."

Matthew 18:21-22 ESV

Learning how to forgive requires practice—and lots of it. So when it comes to forgiveness, here's something you should remember: even if your feelings are still upset, don't give up!

Are you having trouble forgiving someone for a mistake? Or maybe someone keeps doing the same wrong thing to you over and over? If so, remember that forgiveness is a choice and you can keep choosing it until you don't have those mad or sad feelings anymore. Don't forget to ask God to help you forgive others.

THOUGHT OF THE DAY

When we need to forgive, it helps to remember that God forgives us.

PRAY TODAY

Dear God, You have forgiven me—a lot. Please help me practice forgiveness today. Amen.

a Bright Light

"You are the light of the world. A city situated on a hill cannot be hidden."

Matthew 5:14 HCSB

Have you ever thought about the fact that people are watching what you do and how you live? Maybe you have a little brother or sister who looks up to you. Or maybe it could be the neighbors next door or your friends at school or even their parents.

What do others see when they look at you? If you love God and live your life doing what is right, then you can't help but show them how much God loves them. That's how you can be a bright light to the whole world.

THOUGHT OF THE DAY

God created you to be a light to everyone around you, so shine bright in all you do!

PRAY TODAY

Dear God, help me to be more like You so I can shine brightly. I want others to see Jesus in me. Amen.

Give it to God

Since God assured us, "I'll never let you down, never walk off and leave you," we can boldly quote, God is there, ready to help; I'm fearless no matter what. Who or what can get to me?

Hebrews 13:5-6 MSG

D o you have a problem that you can't figure out? There is only one thing you need to do: turn that problem over to God. He can handle it!

God has a way of solving our problems for us if we let Him–nothing is impossible for Him! If you're worried or discouraged, pray about it. Ask your parents and friends to pray about it, too. Then give it to God and stop worrying, because no problem is too big for Him; not even yours!

THOUGHT OF THE DAY

If something is bothering you, write a note to God and ask for his help.

PRAY TODAY

Dear God, I am so glad there is no problem that is too big for You. Thank You for helping me with mine. Amen.

a Lot of Listening

A fool's way is right in his own eyes, but whoever listens to counsel is wise.

Proverbs 12:15 HCSB

Directions, directions, directions. It seems like somebody is always giving you directions: telling you where to go, how to behave, and what to do next. Sometimes, all these directions can be confusing! How can you understand everything that everybody tells you?

The answer, of course, is that you must pay careful attention and that means listening. A lot. And if you aren't sure about what you've heard the first time, don't be afraid to ask questions!

THOUGHT OF THE DAY

Things almost always go wrong if you don't listen to directions.

PRAY TODAY

Dear God, sometimes it is hard to hear everything I need to. Help me become a better listener. Amen.

Friends You Can Trust

Friends come and friends go, but a true friend sticks by you like family.

Proverbs 18:24 MSG

Friendships that last a long time have both honesty and trust. A true friend is someone you can always count on—no matter what. They always tell you the truth and always stick by you when trouble comes.

Do you want to have friends you can trust? A faithful friend is hard to find! Start by being honest and trustworthy yourself. Next, spend your time with friends who like you for who you really are. After a while, you will have friends that feel like they are a part of your family.

THOUGHT OF THE DAY

The best way to make a friend is to be one.

PRAY TODAY

Dear God, thank You for good friends I can trust. Let me be a trustworthy person and a good friend. Amen.

GENTLE WORDS

Always be humble, gentle, and patient, accepting each other in love.

Ephesians 4:2 NCV

The Bible tells us that gentle words are helpful and loving. But sometimes, especially when we're upset, our words and our actions may not be so nice. Sometimes, we may say things that are unkind or hurtful to others.

It is never a good idea to say hurtful things. It might make you feel better for a moment, but soon you will feel bad and so will the other person! The next time you're tempted to say something you shouldn't, don't. Remember–gentle words are always better than angry words!

THOUGHT OF THE DAY

God doesn't want us to spread words that hurt, he wants us to spread nice words.

PRAY TODAY

Dear God, the Bible teaches me to be gentle and kind. So, I will do my best to treat other people just like I want to be treated. Amen.

Be a Happy Giver

God loves the person who gives happily.

2 Corinthians 9:7 ICB

One of the best ways to learn to follow God is by sharing your time, effort and things with others. You will be amazed at the wonderful things that can happen! But it is important that you remember God wants you to give "happily." That means giving with a kind heart and without wanting to withhold your best or expecting something in return.

Make a habit of giving just because you want to help someone. There is nothing like making others happy–the joy is contagious!

THOUGHT OF THE DAY

It is truly better to give than to receive.

PRAY TODAY

Dear God, I want to share my blessings with my family, with my friends, and with people who need my help. Amen.

On The Inside

God does not see the same way people see. People look at the outside of a person, but the Lord looks at the heart.

1 Samuel 16:7 NCV

O ther people see you from the outside, and they may judge you based on the way you look. But God looks at things differently. Why? Because He cares about who you are on the inside–God sees your heart.

That doesn't mean you shouldn't try to look your best. But don't let what you look like on the outside determine how you think about yourself. God made you special and there is no one else in the whole world like you! Don't compare yourself to others or worry about how you look. God thinks you are wonderful just the way He made you!

THOUGHT OF THE DAY
What are some things about you that are special?

PRAY TODAY
Dear God, You said it's what's inside my heart that matters most. Help me pay more attention to the inside, too. Amen.

Perfect Love

For God so loved the world that he gave his only Son, so that everyone who believes in him will not perish but have eternal life.

John 3:16 NLT

The Bible makes this promise: God is love. It's a big promise, and a very important one that tells us who and what God is and how He works.

God's love is perfect. Even the people who love you the most will make mistakes from time to time, and hurt your feelings. All kinds of things can go wrong, but God's love will never fail you. He would do anything for you. He loves you now and forever. That's why He sent Jesus so you could be saved. With a love like that, there is nothing for you to worry about!

THOUGHT OF THE DAY

God made you special and He loves you very much!

PRAY TODAY

Dear God, thank You for loving me so much and in every way that is perfect. Amen.

a Wise King

If you need wisdom–if you want to know what God wants you to do–ask him, and he will gladly tell you.

James 1:5 NLT

Solomon wasn't just a king. He was also a very wise man–the wisest man who ever lived! What was the most important advice he wrote in the Bible? He said, "Honor God and obey His commandments."

The next time you have an important choice to make, ask yourself this: "Am I honoring God and obeying Him? And am I doing what God would want me to do?" As long as you ask God for wisdom and do your best to follow it, you have nothing to worry about!

THOUGHT OF THE DAY

What is one important thing you have to make a choice about every day?

PRAY TODAY

Dear God, there are so many choices for me to make. Please help me choose wisely. Amen.

STRONG AND WONDERFUL!

The Lord your God is God of all gods and Lord of all lords. He is the great God, who is strong and wonderful.

Deuteronomy 10:17 NCV

In the story of Gideon in the Bible, God helped Gideon defeat the Midianites with only a handful of men and some pretty strange "weapons."

Gideon was able to trust God completely because he knew that God is strong enough to do anything. And wonderful enough to win a battle with a bunch of horns and lanterns, if that is what it takes!

If you trust God, you will see Him do wonderful things through you, too!

THOUGHT OF THE DAY

Read the story of Gideon in Judges, chapters 6-7. How did God turn trust into victory?

PRAY TODAY

Dear God, it must have been pretty exciting to win a battle with horns and lights! I can't wait to see what other great things You will do! Amen.

WHAT YOU THINK YOU KNOW

The words of a gossip are like tasty bits of food. People like to gobble them up.

Proverbs 18:8 NCV

What is gossip? It's when you talk about people. And if you aren't careful, the words you say can hurt someone's feelings or cause a lot of trouble.

Sometimes you can gossip and not even realize what you are doing. Junior and Laura learned this the hard way. They weren't trying to be mean or say unkind words. They were just talking. But words can spread fast and can make a really big mess.

So remember to always pay attention to what you say, and do your best to only say what is good.

THOUGHT OF THE DAY

A smart rule to live by: If you can't think of something nice to say, don't say anything.

PRAY TODAY

Dear God, I know words can hurt. Please help me pay close attention to what I say and only speak kind words. Amen.

Yes, You Can!

But Jesus looked at them and said, "With men this is impossible, but with God all things are possible."

Matthew 19:26 HCSB

Lots of people in the world will tell you that you "can't." You "can't"-that thing is too hard. You "can't"-nobody else has ever made that dream come true. You "can't"-it's just not possible. There's always a reason they say you "can't."

But the good news is that with God you "can." What seems impossible to someone else is totally possible with God! That means there is nothing you can't accomplish, if you trust God and do what He says.

God says, "Yes, you can!"

THOUGHT OF THE DAY
Do you have a dream? Write it down and pray about it.

PRAY TODAY
Dear God, help me find the things that You want me to do and a way to do it. Amen.

SHOWING KINDNESS

I tell you the truth, anything you did for even the least of my people here, you also did for me.

Matthew 25:40 NCV

The Bible says that when we do something kind or help someone in need, it is as though we were doing those things for Jesus.

That means that when you help your friend with their homework, or take a meal to a sick neighbor, or offer to help your mom clean the house, that you are being kind to Jesus. And He always appreciates it!

So don't worry if someone isn't kind back, just keep doing what you can and God will take care of the rest.

THOUGHT OF THE DAY

Being kind is about showing people how much God loves them.

PRAY TODAY

Dear God, I want to make You happy, Lord, so I will keep helping others. Amen.

GOD WILL MAKE THINGS RIGHT

God is fair and just; He corrects the misdirected, sends them in the right direction.

Psalm 25:8 MSG

God always knows what He's doing, and He never makes a mistake. On the other hand, you will probably make mistakes occasionally. We all do!

The good news is that God is full of mercy. And when we get off-track, He always puts us back on the right path with love and kindness.

So don't worry. If you make a mistake and need help, just ask for His help and forgiveness. Then trust God to work out whatever needs to be made right. He's got it covered!

THOUGHT OF THE DAY

Any time you need help—just ask God. He loves you and is quick to answer.

PRAY TODAY

Dear God, when I make a mistake, thank You for giving me mercy and making things right. Amen.

Love Your Enemy

"There is a saying, 'Love your friends and hate your enemies.' But I say: Love your enemies! Pray for those who persecute you!"

Matthew 5:43-44 TLB

Jesus said we should love our enemies. Can you imagine that? Sometimes it is hard enough to love your little sister or brother, but your enemy?! That seems like too much to expect!

But God knows that loving others–even your enemies–can change any situation. What do you think God could do if you loved your enemy? Maybe if you show them kindness, your enemy might become your friend. Or maybe they will want to know God. So forgive them and show them God's love. A miracle could happen!

THOUGHT OF THE DAY
Showing love to your enemies is being like Jesus.

PRAY TODAY
Dear God, help me remember to show kindness even to those who don't treat me kindly. Amen.

Practice Patience

And to your knowledge, add self-control; and to your self-control, add patience.

2 Peter 1:6 NCV

How hard is it to be a patient person? Very, very, very hard–sometimes it may even seem impossible. But God wants us to learn patience anyway!

Being patient is hard for everybody–for kids and grownups, too. So don't get upset with yourself if you have a hard time being patient. Just keep working at it. Like lots of important things, it takes some practice.

If God says we need patience, He must have a good reason. So keep trying!

THOUGHT OF THE DAY

Ask your parents to help you remember to be patient. And when they remind you–take a deep breath and count to ten!

PRAY TODAY

Dear God, thank You for helping me become more patient. I know it is worth the effort. Amen.

JUST ASK!

When doubts filled my mind, your comfort gave me renewed hope and cheer.

Psalm 94:19 NLT

When you're not sure about something, are you willing to ask questions about what you should do? Hopefully, when you have a question, you're not afraid to speak up and ask.

If you've got lots of questions, the Bible promises that God has all the answers you need.

So don't ever be afraid to ask. Your parents and teachers and your Heavenly Father want to hear your questions . . . and do everything they can to help you. Just ask!

THOUGHT OF THE DAY

If you're not sure whether or not something is right or wrong, ask your parents before you do it!

PRAY TODAY

Dear God, thank You for giving me the courage to ask questions when I need answers. Amen.

Believe in Yourself

As Goliath moved closer to attack, David quickly ran out to meet him.

1 Samuel 17:48 NLT

David was the baby brother. He was the young kid who just took care of the sheep. Nobody expected him to be the one to kill Goliath, or to become king of Israel. But he did.

The good news is God doesn't see you as "too little" or "too young." He knows what you can become, if you will just trust Him and believe in yourself.

Don't let what other people say determine your future. If God says you can do it–you can!

THOUGHT OF THE DAY
With God's help, little guys can do big things too!

PRAY TODAY
Dear God, You say that I can do big things! So I will believe You, and believe in myself, and I will do my best. Amen.

SHARE GOD'S LOVE

If you have two shirts, share with the person who does not have one. If you have food, share that too.

Luke 3:11 ICB

God talks a lot about sharing and giving in the Bible. It's really important to Him that we take care of each other–especially those who don't have everything they need, like food and clothing and a safe place to live.

You may not think you can make a big difference–but you can! If you ask God to show you how you can share with others, He will show you what to do.

Even a small act of kindness can change a person's life. Share God's love everywhere you go!

THOUGHT OF THE DAY

Who do you know–either a grownup or a kid–that could use your help?

PRAY TODAY

Dear God, I want to do whatever I can to help people and show them how much You love them. Amen.

WATCH OUT!

"Stay awake and pray for strength against temptation. The spirit wants to do what is right, but the body is weak."

Matthew 26:41 NCV

How do you beat temptation? Watch for it . . . and when it comes, run the other way!

Everybody is tempted to do things that are wrong. But one of the best ways to be happy (and stay that way) is to learn how to resist temptation.

You probably know what tempts you the most. The smart thing to do is to watch out for that temptation and have a plan. Ask God and your parents to help you, and when temptation comes–run the other way!

THOUGHT OF THE DAY

Think of three things you can do when you are tempted and write them down. Now you have a plan!

PRAY TODAY

Dear God, please help me remember to run away from temptation and not give in. Amen.

David was Brave!

"Don't worry about this Philistine," David told Saul. "I'll go fight him!"

1 Samuel 17:32 NLT

D o you know the story of David and Goliath? Goliath was saying all kinds of bad things about God and God's people, and no one would do anything about it. They were all too scared to move because he was gigantic and mean.

David couldn't believe his ears! Even though no one else would fight Goliath, David did. He knew that when something needs to be done, the best time to do it is now, not later.

When you see something that isn't right, be brave and do something about it!

THOUGHT OF THE DAY

When you're brave and trust God, hard things become easier.

PRAY TODAY

Dear God, please help me be brave when I need to do a hard thing. I know You will help me. Amen.

a Win-Win

*Be gentle with one another, sensitive. Forgive one another
as quickly and thoroughly as God in Christ forgave you.*

Ephesians 4:32 MSG

How hard is it to forgive people? Sometimes, it's very hard! But God tells us that we must forgive, even when we'd rather think about how much our feelings are hurt. Or even worse, how we could get even.

The Bible also tells us to treat other people the way we want to be treated. And we all need to be forgiven sometimes. When you forgive, you are obeying God and also choosing how you want others to treat you. It's a win-win for everybody!

THOUGHT OF THE DAY

Are you having a hard time forgiving someone? Think of something really big that God has forgiven you for.

PRAY TODAY

Dear God, sometimes forgiving is really hard. But I will forgive and keep forgiving, just like You always forgive me. Amen.

a Good attitude

Set your minds on what is above, not on what is on the earth.

Colossians 3:2 HCSB

Larry has learned that attitude is really important–it can make you feel happy or sad, joyful or mad. How do you have a good attitude? It starts with how you think. If you think about good things, it's easy to see the good things around you. But if you always think about bad stuff, you can find plenty of that, too.

If you "set your mind" on God, which means you choose to think about Him, and remember the great things He has done for you, it's easy to have a good attitude. Choose to think about good things today!

THOUGHT OF THE DAY

Remember that every day you can choose to have a good attitude!

PRAY TODAY

Dear God, help me remember that my attitude makes all the difference and to think about good things today. Amen.

a LiTTLe encouragement

So encourage each other and give each other strength....

1 Thessalonians 5:11 NCV

We all need a little encouragement once in a while. Sometimes, the best thing might be a kind word or help solving a problem. Many people just need someone to listen.

What can you do to cheer up your friends when they are feeling sad? Maybe you goof around or tell a joke. Maybe you sing a silly song! Sometimes, the only thing you can do is just be there. But however you express it, do your best to show kindness and love. That's the best encouragement of all!

THOUGHT OF THE DAY

If your friend is lonely or going through a hard time, spend some extra time with them and pray for them.

PRAY TODAY

Dear God, please help me find ways to encourage my family and friends whenever I can. Amen.

Celebrate Every Day!

This is the day that the Lord has made. Let us rejoice and be glad today!

Psalm 118:24 NCV

The Bible tells us that we should rejoice and be glad every day! After all, this day (like every other day) has unlimited opportunities–anything can happen!

You probably are used to celebrating special occasions like birthdays and holidays. But even on "regular" days, there is always something to be excited about and celebrate. For one, God loves you very much and has given you many, many things to be thankful for.

Don't miss your chance to celebrate today–remember to thank God and rejoice!

THOUGHT OF THE DAY

God is just as excited about today as you are about your birthday!

PRAY TODAY

Dear God, I will celebrate today–if for no other reason than because You love me! Amen.

WHY DO BAD THINGS HAPPEN?

He comes alongside us when we go through hard times, and before you know it, he brings us alongside someone else who is going through hard times so that we can be there for that person just as God was there for us.

2 Corinthians 1:4 MSG

If God is good, why do bad things happen? Sometimes, bad things happen because people choose not to listen to God. He always wants the best for us, and not listening to His guidance will usually bring sadness and trouble into our lives.

Other times, bad things happen, and it's nobody's fault. Sometimes, we just don't know why. But the Bible promises us that when we go through hard times, that God is right there beside us. He can bring us through anything—no matter how bad it might seem.

THOUGHT OF THE DAY

Have you seen something bad that happened on the news? If so, talk to your parents and tell them how it made you feel.

PRAY TODAY

Dear God, I don't always understand why bad things happen, but when they do I will trust You. Amen.

Don't Be Jealous

Jealousy will rot your bones.

Proverbs 14:30 NCV

Sometimes, you might feel jealous of others–of the fun things they get to do or of the stuff they have. Especially if they have something you really like. But God doesn't want you to envy anybody. He wants you to be thankful for what you have.

Why? Because if all you think about is what other people have, you will never be happy. The Bible says "jealousy will rot your bones." Wow! That sounds pretty awful!

Be happy for others and thankful for what you have– and you will be happy, too!

THOUGHT OF THE DAY
If you are feeling a little jealous of a friend, pray and thank God for blessing them.

PRAY TODAY
Dear God, I don't want to be jealous. Help me have a thankful and happy heart. Amen.

Choose Wisely

I am offering you life or death, blessings or curses. Now, choose life! . . . To choose life is to love the Lord your God, obey him, and stay close to him.

Deuteronomy 30:19-20 NCV

Choices, choices, choices! You have so many choices to make, and sometimes, they aren't easy. Sometimes you might have to choose between what you want to do and what you should do. When that happens, it's up to you to choose wisely.

When you make good choices, there is always a reward–sometimes in what doesn't happen. When you make unwise choices, there are consequences that will come that may be hard to deal with. It's as simple as that. So choose God and choose life!

THOUGHT OF THE DAY

Have you made a choice that you knew wasn't what God wanted you to do? What happened?

PRAY TODAY

Dear God, I have many choices to make today. Help me choose wisely and do what You want me to. Amen.

FIGHT FEAR

For God has not given us a spirit of fear, but of power and of love and of a sound mind.

2 Timothy 1:7 NKJV

Fear is a powerful force—it can paralyze you, or keep you from doing things you want to do, or worse, steal your happiness and joy.

But fear is never from God and He doesn't want you to let it win. In fact, God gives you three amazing weapons to fight fear: Power, Love, and a Sound Mind.

The Power of God is greater than anything that could ever come against you. His Love overcomes every evil thing. And He gives you a Sound Mind—or the ability to think clearly—in every situation.

So use your weapons and fight fear today!

THOUGHT OF THE DAY

If you are afraid of something, talk about it with your parents.

PRAY TODAY

Dear God, sometimes I get so afraid I can hardly breathe. Help me remember to use Your weapons to fight fear. Amen.

Peace at Home

My dear brothers, always be willing to listen and slow to speak. Do not become angry easily. Anger will not help you live a good life as God wants.

James 1:19 ICB

Sometimes, it's easy to become angry with the people we love most, and sometimes it's hardest to forgive them. After all, we know that our family will still love us no matter what we do. But staying mad with your family can cause big problems.

The next time you get angry at a parent or sibling, remember that these are the people who love you more than anybody else! Then, calm down and choose your words carefully. Most of all, make sure to forgive them! Because peace is always best, especially when it's peace at your house.

THOUGHT OF THE DAY

Think about a time when your family forgave you. How did that make you feel?

PRAY TODAY

Dear God, if I become angry with my family, help me to forgive them quickly. Help me do my part to keep peace and love in my house. Amen.

No More Fighting

It's a mark of good character to avert quarrels, but fools love to pick fights.

Proverbs 20:3 MSG

Have you ever noticed how easy it is to get into an argument? When two people disagree about something, things can quickly get out of hand. Sometimes, people will try to start a fight–either by hitting or saying awful, hurtful words.

But nothing good can come out of a fight. And God loves it when you can find ways to stop a fight before it starts. The Bible says fools love to start a fight . . . but you don't have to argue or fight back. You are no fool!

THOUGHT OF THE DAY

What are some ways to avoid fighting and arguing? Can you walk away? Say something funny? What else?

PRAY TODAY

Dear God, help me remember to be kind and do my best to avoid arguments and fights. Amen.

We all need Forgiveness

If you forgive others for the wrongs they do to you, your Father in heaven will forgive you.

Matthew 6:14 CEV

The Bible tells us that it is important to forgive, even when we don't really want to, so that God can forgive us.

Sometimes our feelings are really, really hurt and it may seem impossible to forgive. That's when you choose to do it anyway. After all, hasn't God forgiven you for some pretty big things?

If you are having trouble forgiving, just ask for God's help and He will give it to you. We all need forgiveness–all the time.

THOUGHT OF THE DAY

Decide to forgive and do it quickly . . . then don't dwell on what happened. Just let it go.

PRAY TODAY

Dear God, sometimes it's very hard to forgive those who have hurt me, but I want to forgive others just as You have already forgiven me. Amen.

BRING OUT THE BEST

Look for the best in each other, and always do your best to bring it out.

1 Thessalonians 5:15 MSG

Your friends and family are a special gift from God. It is wonderful to have people who love and support you, and it's important to do all you can do to love and support them back!

Tho Bible says we should "look for the best in each other." That means instead of getting angry, or complaining and criticizing, focus on what makes them special.

You can bring out the best in them by giving encouraging words, thanking them for the ways they help you, and doing whatever you can to help them make their dreams come true!

THOUGHT OF THE DAY

When your friend makes a mistake or upsets you, think of something kind that they have done for you.

PRAY TODAY

Dear God, nobody is perfect! Please help me remember that and to always look for the good in people. Amen.

a Forever Love

The unfailing love of the Lord never ends!

Lamentations 3:22 NLT

How much does God love you? So much that He sent His Son Jesus to Earth for you! So much that because of Jesus, you can have the greatest gift of all–a forever life with God in heaven.

God's love is bigger and more powerful than anybody can imagine, but it is very real. His love for you is forever and will never fail. So tell God that you love Him too, and ask Jesus to come into your heart. When you do, He'll show you how much He loves you.

THOUGHT OF THE DAY

God loves you so much you can trust Him with anything! Always!

PRAY TODAY

Dear God, thank You for loving me. I want to know You better and have that forever kind of love. Amen.

LOOK FOR THE GOOD THINGS

Dear friend, do not imitate what is evil, but what is good. The one who does good is of God; the one who does evil has not seen God.

3 John 1:11 HCSB

I f you look for the good in other people, you'll probably find it. And, if you look for the good things in your life, you'll probably find them, too.

When you start looking for good things, you'll find them everywhere: in church, at school, in your neighborhood, and at home.

So don't waste your time on things that make you feel angry, discouraged, worried, guilty, or afraid. Instead, look for the things that God wants you to pay attention to—no matter how small they might seem.

THOUGHT OF THE DAY

Can you think of three good things that God has given you?

PRAY TODAY

Dear God, help me to always think good thoughts and look for the best in other people. Amen.

Be Happy

I will be happy because of you; God Most High, I will sing praises to your name.

Psalm 9:2 NCV

Did you know that you can choose to be happy—even if things don't seem to be going the way you want them to? It's true!

The Bible says we can be happy because of God—not because of the things that happen to us. Happiness comes from loving God and having a thankful heart.

God never changes and He has done so many great things for you. So make the choice to praise God and thank Him today, instead of worrying about what might go wrong. With God, every day can be a happy one!

THOUGHT OF THE DAY

A thankful heart is a happy heart! What are you thankful for today?

PRAY TODAY

Dear God, thank You for everything You have done for me. I will choose to be happy today. Amen.

a Lie is a Lie

Since you put away lying, speak the truth, each one to his neighbor, because we are members of one another.

Ephesians 4:25 HCSB

Sometimes people tell themselves that it's okay to tell fibs or "little white lies." They think that "itsy bitsy" lies aren't harmful, especially if they can help get you out of a difficult situation. But there's a problem: little lies have a way of growing into big ones, and once they grow, they can cause a lot of problems.

God wants us to be truthful with each other. Of course, kindness sometimes requires that we just don't say anything at all. But in God's eyes, the size of the lie doesn't matter at all. A lie is a lie is a lie.

THOUGHT OF THE DAY

If you always tell the truth, you won't have to worry about what you said!

PRAY TODAY

Dear God, help me to always tell the truth . . . even with the little things. Amen.

PUT OTHERS FIRST

Don't be selfish. . . . Be humble, thinking of others as better than yourself.

Philippians 2:3 TLB

Being humble means putting others first and showing people how much God loves them by how we treat them.

Jesus was perfect in every way–there has never been anyone as important as Him! But everywhere He went, He took care of people who needed help, and He always thought of others before Himself.

One thing is for sure . . . when we only think about ourselves, we miss a chance to share God's love. Selfishness always leads to unhappiness, but being humble and sharing God's love makes everything better!

THOUGHT OF THE DAY

Putting others first is always the best thing to do–even if that means you don't always get what you want.

PRAY TODAY

Dear God, help me remember to put others first today. I want to live my life like Jesus did. Amen.

a Joyful Heart

A joyful heart is good medicine.

Proverbs 17:22 HCSB

God doesn't want us to spend our days moping around with frowns on our faces. Far from it! God wants you to have a joyful heart.

The Bible says that a joyful heart is like medicine—it makes you and everyone around you feel better.

God wants you to laugh and be silly! Work hard at school and get your chores and homework done, but don't forget to spend time doing things you love with your friends and family. You were made to have fun, dance around, and laugh out loud!

THOUGHT OF THE DAY

Nothing feels as good as laughing until your belly hurts.

PRAY TODAY

Dear God, thank You for the gift of laughter. It's fun and makes everything better. Help me laugh today! Amen.

The Good Samaritan

Never walk away from someone who deserves help; your hand is God's hand for that person.

Proverbs 3:27 MSG

Sometimes we want to help make the world a better place, but we aren't sure how to do it.

Jesus told the story of the "Good Samaritan," a man who helped a fellow traveler who was hurt when no one else would. What made the difference? When he saw someone in trouble, the Good Samaritan didn't ignore the problem and did what he could to help.

There are always people who need help. You can find them at home, at school, and at church. Just keep your eyes open and do what you can!

THOUGHT OF THE DAY

When you love your neighbor, loving means lending a hand!

PRAY TODAY

Dear God, let me keep my eyes open to look for people who need help. Thank You for using me. Amen.

Stay Connected

"Yes, I am the Vine; you are the branches. Whoever lives in me and I in him shall produce a large crop of fruit. For apart from me you can't do a thing."

John 15:5 TLB

The Bible tells us that Jesus is the Vine and we are the branches. Without food, nutrients, and water from the main vine, the branches and leaves on a plant will die. That means that everything we need comes from Him.

It is important to remember that without God, we can do nothing. But when we stay connected to Him, we can "produce a large crop of fruit." In other words, we can do lots of amazing things!

THOUGHT OF THE DAY

How does Jesus give you what you need to live?

PRAY TODAY

Dear God, thank You for giving me everything I need to live my life. Amen.

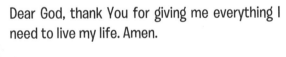

Be Kind To Everybody

Be kind to one another, tenderhearted, forgiving one another, as God in Christ forgave you.

Ephesians 4:32 ESV

God wants you to do your best to treat everybody with kindness. That can be hard sometimes, especially when people may not be very nice to you. But that's how God wants you to treat others so they will see how much He loves them, too.

If someone says something to you that isn't very nice, try not to pay too much attention or worry about it. Just forgive them as quickly as you can, and keep being patient and kind. God will take care of it!

THOUGHT OF THE DAY

Is there someone you know who makes it really hard to be kind? Take a minute and pray for them.

PRAY TODAY

Dear God, please help me be kind today. When other people upset me, help me to calm down and forgive them as quickly as I can. Amen.

Listen Up!

Wise people can also listen and learn.

Proverbs 1:5 NCV

Some of the best advice God gives us in the Bible is to be quick to hear. Why? Because if we pay attention and listen, we can avoid a lot of problems and misunderstandings in life. But when you're frustrated or tired, it's easy to speak first and think later.

A big part of growing up is learning how to slow down long enough to listen to the things that people have to say to you. Even if you don't like what you hear, do your best to be slow to speak and slow to get angry.

So the next time someone is talking, show them you care, listen up!

THOUGHT OF THE DAY

If someone is talking to you, look them in the eyes so they know you are listening.

PRAY TODAY

Dear God, I have a lot to learn. Help me to watch and listen first, before I speak. Amen.

a Love That Lasts Forever

I am the good shepherd. The good shepherd lays down his life for the sheep.

John 10:11 NIV

Do you sometimes wonder how much Jesus loves you? Jesus loves you so much that He gave His life so that you might live forever with Him in heaven. There is nothing He wouldn't do for you and He loves you just the way you are—with the good stuff and the not-so-good. And His love lasts forever. He will never change His mind about you.

How do you receive Jesus' love? By accepting Him into your heart, spending time with Him, and getting to know Him more each day. Your life will never be the same!

THOUGHT OF THE DAY

Jesus is full of kindness and love. He will never betray you.

PRAY TODAY

Dear God, thank You for Your Son, Jesus, and for His great love for me. Amen.

Too Much Stuff

Don't be obsessed with getting more material things. Be relaxed with what you have.

Hebrews 13:5 MSG

Here's something to remember about stuff: It's really not very important!

Lots of people spend all their time thinking about money and all the things that money can buy. But God cares about people, not possessions. In fact, the Bible tells us that when we go to heaven, we can't take any of that "stuff" with us.

So don't be too concerned about the clothes you wear or the things you own. All of that stuff will wear out eventually, but your relationships with God, your family, and your friends are forever!

THOUGHT OF THE DAY

If you only focus on stuff, you will miss out on all the best things in life.

PRAY TODAY

Dear God, help me think more about people and less about the things I want to own. Amen.

CHOOSE TO OBEY

Now, Israel, listen to the laws and commands I will teach you. Obey them so that you will live.

Deuteronomy 4:1 NCV

D o you know why God talks so much about obeying in the Bible? Because He always has a plan, and He needs us to do our part!

Gideon had a choice. When the angel came and told Gideon to go save the children of Israel from their enemies, Gideon could have said no. He could have said God's plan was crazy, or foolish, or impossible. But he didn't. He just obeyed and God saved His people.

You can choose to obey, too. When you do, great things can happen!

THOUGHT OF THE DAY

Why do you think God wants you to obey your parents?

PRAY TODAY

Dear God, sometimes obeying is hard. Please help me to do better. Amen.

Never Give Up!

The Lord says, "Forget what happened before, and do not think about the past. Look at the new thing I am going to do. It is already happening. Don't you see it?"

Isaiah 43:18-19 NCV

No matter how much you try, you can't be a perfect person . . . and that's okay.

God doesn't expect you to live a mistake-free life–and neither should you. God wants you to try your best, but He knows that sometimes you will fail. The important thing is that you should never give up!

So remember this: you don't have to be perfect. In fact, you don't even need to be "almost-perfect." Just keep trying and leave the rest up to God.

THOUGHT OF THE DAY

Don't be too hard on yourself: God loves you just the way you are.

PRAY TODAY

Dear God, help me remember that I don't have to be perfect. I'll do my best and let You take care of the rest. Amen.

a Happy Sacrifice

So through Jesus let us always offer to God our sacrifice of praise, coming from lips that speak his name.

Hebrews 13:15 NCV

The Bible is full of songs of praise and talks a lot about the importance of thanking and praising God. But sometimes, we may not feel like thanking anybody, not even our Father in heaven.

In those moments, we should offer a "sacrifice" of praise. Meaning we do it because it is the right thing to do, not because of how we feel.

The big surprise though, is that once we start to praise God, it doesn't take long before we feel a lot better. Happiness comes from praising our Father!

THOUGHT OF THE DAY

Whenever you have a problem, the best thing to do first is to praise God.

PRAY TODAY

Dear God, You are amazing and wonderful and I am Yours. Thank You for filling my heart with praise to You. Amen.

PRAY ABOUT IT!

For the eyes of the Lord are over the righteous, and his ears are open unto their prayers.

1 Peter 3:12 KJV

Is something bothering you today? Pray about it! Is there something that has made you sad or worried? Pray about it! Do you wish you could do better in school? Pray about it! Do you struggle with self-control and wish you could do better? Then pray about it!

No matter what the situation or problem, whenever you pray about something, God hears your prayer . . . and He can always help. So don't worry about things or let them bother you; pray about them. God is waiting . . . and listening!

THOUGHT OF THE DAY

Prayer always changes things!

PRAY TODAY

Dear God, thank You for loving me and for always being ready to listen when I pray. Help me remember I can talk to You about everything. Amen.

You're So Very Special

For I know you well and you are special to me. I know you by name.

Exodus 33:17 MSG

When God made you, He made you in a very special way. In fact, you're a wonderful, one-of-a-kind creation; a special person unlike any other.

Do you realize how important you are to God? Do you know that God's feelings for you are based on who you are–not the things you've done (either good or bad) or where you come from? And do you know that God has important things for you to do?

All these things are all true . . . so be glad that you are you!

THOUGHT OF THE DAY

Remember, if you get frustrated with yourself . . . God's not finished with you yet!

PRAY TODAY

Dear God, thank You for making me a special person and for loving me. Amen.

Kindness is a Choice

Love is patient; love is kind.

1 Corinthians 13:4 HCSB

Sometimes, when we are feeling happy or hopeful, it can feel easy to be kind. Other times, when we are sad or tired, we may find it much harder to think about others. But the Bible teaches us to be kind, even when we don't feel like it.

Do your best to be kind to others all the time. Kindness is one of the ways we show God's love, and a little kindness can really make a big difference in someone's life! You really can do it–because kindness is a choice!

THOUGHT OF THE DAY

Kindness is in the little things. Find something you can do to help your mom clean up today.

PRAY TODAY

Dear God, help me to show kindness to the people I meet, and lend a helping hand whenever I can. Amen.

Difficult Days

"If you'll hold on to me for dear life," says God, "I'll get you out of any trouble. I'll give you the best of care if you'll only get to know and trust me. Call me and I'll answer, be at your side in bad times; I'll rescue you, then throw you a party."

Psalm 91:14-15 MSG

et's face it: some days are better than others. But even on the days when everything seems to go wrong, God never leaves you for even a moment. So if you need Him, you can always pray, knowing that He will listen and help.

If you're feeling unhappy, talk things over with God, and while you're at it, be sure and talk things over with your parents, too. You can be certain that things will get better . . . because He promised to take care of you. And nothing is impossible for God!

THOUGHT OF THE DAY

When life is hard, God wants us to remember to pray and trust Him.

PRAY TODAY

Dear God, when I'm having a hard day, I'll turn to You and ask for help. I know that things will get better soon. Amen.

act on it!

But prove yourselves doers of the word, and not merely hearers.

James 1:22 NASB

D o you sometimes listen to what your parents tell you, but then don't do what they say? How does that usually work out? Probably not very well.

Your relationship with God is the same way. If you listen to what He says in the Bible, and believe what you learn at church to be true, but don't act like it, the results will not be very good.

Hearing what God has to say to you is the first step. Acting on it is the second. When you do, God will honor your good choices, and your good choices will honor God.

THOUGHT OF THE DAY

Do what Junior Asparagus does and stand up for what you believe in.

PRAY TODAY

Dear God, please help me to listen to what You have to say and then do it! Amen.

DON'T WORRY . . . TRUST GOD

The Lord himself will go before you. He will be with you; he will not leave you or forget you. Don't be afraid and don't worry.

Deuteronomy 31:8 NCV

Do you worry a lot about what might happen to you? If so, you aren't alone. Lots of people struggle with worry-grownups and kids alike.

But God tells us in the Bible-over and over-not to worry or be afraid. Why? Because God wants us to trust Him. After all, He is in control and can handle anything that happens. He also loves you and has promised to never leave you or forget about you.

So what's the point of worrying? Worry can't change anything . . . it just makes you unhappy. Instead, trust God and relax!

THOUGHT OF THE DAY

When you feel afraid or start to worry, sing your favorite song from church.

PRAY TODAY

Dear God, I know You don't want me to worry about anything. Help me remember to trust You and relax. Amen.

a Pure Heart

Those with pure hearts shall become stronger and stronger.

Job 17:9 TLB

Have you ever wondered where a good attitude begins? It starts in your heart and grows from there. Jesus taught us that a pure heart is a wonderful gift. When our hearts are full of love for God, love for Jesus, and love for other people, good things happen.

Do you want to be the best person you can be? Then don't give up! Keep thinking about good things and doing the good things for others just because you love God. If you keep your heart right, you will keep growing stronger and stronger in Him.

THOUGHT OF THE DAY

Pray and ask God for a happy and pure heart.

PRAY TODAY

Dear God, please help me keep my heart right so I can have an attitude that pleases You. Amen.

Choices Matter

"Choose this day whom you will serve. . . . But as for me and my house, we will serve the Lord."

Joshua 24:15 ESV

There's really no way to get around it: choices matter. If you make good choices, good things will usually happen. And if you make bad choices, bad things will usually happen.

The next time you have an important decision to make, ask yourself this: "Am I doing what God wants me to do?" If you can say "Yes!" then go ahead. But if you're not sure if the choice you are about to make is right, slow down. Why? Because choices matter . . . and God's way is always best.

THOUGHT OF THE DAY

Choices start off small, but as you grow they become bigger and bigger!

PRAY TODAY

Dear God, help me make good choices today by doing what You would want me to do. Amen.

God's House

For where two or three are gathered together in My name, I am there among them.

Matthew 18:20 HCSB

Do you like to have friends come over and play at your house? Do you like spending time with them? What things do you like to do together?

Church is a wonderful place to learn about God, be with Him, and tell Him how much you love Him. The next time your mom and dad take you to church, remember that you are visiting God's house!

THOUGHT OF THE DAY

Church is important. Thank your mom and dad for taking you there.

PRAY TODAY

Dear God, thanks for letting me come to Your house. Help me pay attention and learn everything I can about You. Amen.

Follow Jesus

"Follow Me," Jesus told them, "and I will make you into fishers of men!" Immediately they left their nets and followed Him.

Mark 1:17-18 HCSB

Following someone means you want to be just like that person. The best person to follow is Jesus!

God's Word says that when you follow Jesus, your life will be changed and blessed forever! You become a brand new person who can do amazing things for God. And then you will live forever in heaven with Jesus! What could be better than that?

THOUGHT OF THE DAY

Don't follow the crowd! Be different . . . and do what's right!

PRAY TODAY

Dear God, I want to follow Jesus every day of my life and tell my family and friends about what He has done for me. Amen.

Lessons To Learn

Remember what you are taught. And listen carefully to words of knowledge.

Proverbs 23:12 ICB

You can learn a lot about life by paying attention to what your parents have to say. Sure, sometimes you may get tired of hearing the same thing over and over. But God gave you parents for a reason–He wants them to teach you what you need to know to live a great life.

You can learn things the easy way, by paying attention and taking their advice, or the hard way, by making the same mistakes over and over again until you finally learn what you should do. So do the wise thing and listen up!

THOUGHT OF THE DAY

When you have a hard decision to make, remember what your parents have taught you!

PRAY TODAY

Dear God, help me listen to my parents and learn the lessons You want me to learn. Amen.

Pray all the Time

Pray constantly. Give thanks in everything, for this is God's will for you in Christ Jesus.

1 Thessalonians 5:17-18 HCSB

Whether you have an outgoing personality or are shy and quiet, there is no reason you can't talk to God all the time. He always wants to listen to what you have to say.

When you pray, you don't have to bow your head and close your eyes. Wherever you are, just start talking to Him like you would talk to your best friend.

THOUGHT OF THE DAY

God is your best friend and always wants to hear from you!

PRAY TODAY

Dear God, help me remember it's always a good time to pray, so I can tell You about the things that are important to me. Amen.

Forgive Them Anyway!

And whenever you stand praying, if you have anything against anyone, forgive him, so that your Father in heaven may also forgive you your wrongdoing.

Mark 11:25 HCSB

The Bible tells us how important it is to forgive people when they hurt us. But what if that person isn't sorry for what they've done to you? What if they never apologize or ask you to forgive them? What do you do?

Forgive them anyway! When you forgive somebody else, you're actually helping yourself. How? Because when you forgive the other person, you get rid of the angry feelings that make you feel unhappy. Your anger hurts you. And God doesn't want you to live that way.

THOUGHT OF THE DAY

You don't need anybody else's permission to forgive. Just go ahead and do it!

PRAY TODAY

Dear God, help me to be quick to forgive all the time, every day; whether anyone asks me to or not. Amen.

a True Friend

There are friends who destroy each other, but a real friend sticks closer than a brother.

Proverbs 19:24 NLT

Everybody needs a good friend–the right kind of friend, anyway! The Bible says that a true friend sticks closer than a brother–no matter what happens, good or bad, they are always there for you.

But if you have a "friend" who hurts you or says mean things to you, they are not really behaving like a friend should. If this happens a lot, you should think about staying away from them. Friends are a wonderful gift from God–when they are good, kind, and truthful!

THOUGHT OF THE DAY

Always try to be the best friend you can be.

PRAY TODAY

Dear God, thank You for my friends who love You and are kind and thoughtful. Amen.

Look Before You Leap

Enthusiasm without knowledge is not good. If you act too quickly, you might make a mistake.

Proverbs 19:2 NCV

D o you sometimes do things without thinking? Do you jump right in before looking where you are going? If so, God wants you to be a little bit more careful—or maybe a lot more careful!

God wants us to behave wisely, not carelessly. If you rush ahead and do things without thinking about them, it's really easy to make big mistakes.

It's worth staying safe by taking a minute to slow down, think things through, and look carefully before you leap.

THOUGHT OF THE DAY

If you're ever not sure about whether you should or shouldn't do something, you can always ask your mom or dad about it.

PRAY TODAY

Dear God, sometimes I'm in too big a hurry. Help me slow down and think about what I'm doing first. Amen.

God Can Handle it

Now the God of all grace, who called you to His eternal glory in Christ Jesus, will personally restore, establish, strengthen, and support you.

1 Peter 5:10 HCSB

It's a promise that is made over and over again in the Bible: No matter what the problem is, God can handle it. We're protected by a loving Heavenly Father.

God can help you when you're sad, He can comfort you. God is right here with you, right now.

There is nothing you need that He won't do for you and no problem He can't fix. So don't worry . . . God's got it all under control!

THOUGHT OF THE DAY

God wants to take care of whatever is bothering you. So talk to Him about it!

PRAY TODAY

Dear God, I know You will take care of me. Help me not to worry when things go wrong and just trust You. Amen.

Rumors and Gossip

Without wood, a fire will go out, and without gossip, quarreling will stop.

Proverbs 26:20 NCV

Have you ever heard your friends talking about other people, saying things that are not very nice, and may or may not be true? That is called gossip.

The Bible tells us not to gossip, for lots of reasons. Rumors and gossip have a way of hurting people's feelings and causing a lot of trouble.

So what can you do? If you hear someone gossiping, try not to listen, ask them to stop saying words that hurt, and definitely don't repeat what they say. Instead, say something kind.

THOUGHT OF THE DAY

Stop gossip in its tracks! Only speak good and kind words about others.

PRAY TODAY

Dear God, I know You hate gossip. Help me to always remember to speak kind words. Amen.

each Day is a Gift

How happy are those who can live in your house, always singing your praises. How happy are those who are strong in the Lord. . . .

Psalm 84:4-5 NLT

God wants you to have a happy, joyful life. But that doesn't mean that you'll be perfectly happy all the time. There will be some days when things will go wrong and you won't feel so great.

When that happens, you can make the choice to be strong and trust in God. If you can hold on when things aren't going so well, before you know it, things will turn around.

When you're feeling a little tired or sad, remember that each new day is a gift from God. Make it the very best day you can!

THOUGHT OF THE DAY

God is with us every day!

PRAY TODAY

Dear God, thank You for today and all of the wonderful things You have done for me. Amen.

Dream for the Future

We can make our plans, but the LORD determines our steps.

Proverbs 16:9 NLT

What do you want to be when you grow up? Do you have a special dream for your future? That's a good thing!

God has a plan that is perfect for you. His very best plans for you will come true as you follow Him.

Just trust Him and wait patiently. It's going to be great!

THOUGHT OF THE DAY

God just wants someone who loves Him with all their heart, and He will take care of the rest.

PRAY TODAY

Dear God, I can't wait to see what will happen in the future. Thank You for helping me. Amen.

a Reason To Hope

May the God of hope fill you with all joy and peace as you trust in him, so that you may overflow with hope by the power of the Holy Spirit.

Romans 15:13 NIV

One of the best things about loving God is that He always gives us a reason to hope—no matter what happens. What is hope? Hope means to expect something with confidence and trust. That is exactly what we are supposed to do as children of God.

God loves you and has promised to take care of you. So no matter what happens, you can expect God to take care of you. He will not let you down!

THOUGHT OF THE DAY

Trusting God is the only way to have real hope.

PRAY TODAY

Dear God, thank You for giving me hope that I can count on. Nothing is too difficult for You! Amen.

Be Kind To Everyone

"I tell you, love your enemies. Help and give without expecting a return. You'll never–I promise–regret it."

Luke 6:35 MSG

It's pretty easy to be nice to people when they are nice to you, but it's not so simple when people treat you badly. Still, the Bible tells us to treat both our friends and our enemies the same–with kindness and respect.

In fact, God says we should love our enemies! That's a pretty big challenge!

Is there someone you know that you really don't like very much? Remember that Jesus not only forgave His enemies, He also loved them . . . and He can help you do the same thing.

THOUGHT OF THE DAY

Sometimes it helps to be prepared. Think of three kind things you can say the next time someone is mean to you.

PRAY TODAY

Dear God, there are some people who make me so mad I can't see straight. But You said I should love them, so I will do my best. Amen.

God's Got a Plan

"Do you think you can explain the mystery of God? Do you think you can diagram God Almighty? God is far higher than you can imagine, far deeper than you can comprehend."

Job 11:7-8 MSG

God told Joshua to defeat Jericho by having the people of Israel march around the walls of the city seven times. Some of God's people thought that sounded crazy. But they obeyed and sure enough, the walls fell down.

Sometimes, it seems impossible to figure out what God is doing–you just can't understand why God would do the things He does. But even when you can't understand God's plan, you can be sure He's got one, and it's good! So just go with it and see what happens!

THOUGHT OF THE DAY

God wants you to trust Him completely!

PRAY TODAY

Dear God, help me remember that you can do anything, even when I don't always understand Your plan. Amen.

Speak the Truth

A witness who lies will not go free; liars will never escape.

Proverbs 19:5 NCV

Sometimes people tell lies, and it may seem like they are going to get away with it. But that doesn't make lying the right thing to do. Far from it. There are always bad consequences for bad choices—even if you can't see them at first.

The important thing for you to remember is that whatever your problem may be, telling a lie is never a good solution. The Bible says that in the end, nobody will get away with lying. So choose God's way and always speak the truth!

THOUGHT OF THE DAY

Whenever you are tempted to lie, stop and remember what God said about telling the truth.

PRAY TODAY

Dear God, help me tell the truth every day of my life. Amen.

Be a God-Pleaser

For am I now trying to win the favor of people, or God? Or am I striving to please people? If I were still trying to please people, I would not be a slave of Christ.

Galatians 1:10 HCSB

Are you a people-pleaser or a God-pleaser? Hopefully, you want to please God more than anyone else. But even if you love God with all your heart, you're still going to feel the urge to impress your friends–and sometimes it will be hard not to go along with what they are doing.

It's your choice: you can choose to please God first, or you can give in to what your friends want. It may not seem like the cool thing to do, but pleasing God is always the best decision. He only wants the very best for you!

THOUGHT OF THE DAY
Look for friends who will help you become a better person.

PRAY TODAY
Dear God, help me remember that I don't have to please everybody . . . but that I should always try to please You! Amen.

a Happy Song

For the LORD your God has arrived to live among you. He is a mighty savior. He will rejoice over you with great gladness. With his love, he will calm all your fears. He will exult over you by singing a happy song.

Zephaniah 3:17 NLT

If God had a refrigerator in heaven, your picture would be on it. Why? Because He's so proud of you and all that you are becoming.

The Bible says He rejoices over you! He sings a happy song, just because He loves watching you grow and learn. He wants to help you become everything He made you to be. Never doubt it–He cares about you!

THOUGHT OF THE DAY

Write a note, sing a song, or draw a picture for God today!

PRAY TODAY

Dear God, thank You for loving me and for caring about everything I do. I want to make You sing for joy! Amen.

Keeping The Peace

How wonderful, how beautiful, when brothers and sisters get along!

Psalm 133:1 MSG

Sometimes your brother or sister can really be hard to get along with.

God wants our families to be loving and kind. Your family loves you more than anybody else! So the next time you get frustrated, calm down and try to be kind. Because it's always wonderful when we get along!

THOUGHT OF THE DAY

With God's help you can be a loving brother or sister.

PRAY TODAY

Dear God, help me love my family and choose to be peaceful, even when they're not perfect. Amen.

Don't Put it Off

We can't afford to waste a minute . . . Get out of bed and get dressed! Don't loiter and linger, waiting until the very last minute. Dress yourselves in Christ, and be up and about!

Romans 13:13-14 MSG

What do you have to do today? Whether you are going to school or staying home for the weekend or planning an activity, there is always plenty to do!

The best way to start each day is to get up out of bed and take care of whatever has to be done. Get dressed and make your bed, have breakfast and do your chores.

Get your work done, then you'll have the rest of your time to have fun!

THOUGHT OF THE DAY

What extra thing can you get done at the end of the day so tomorrow is a little easier?

PRAY TODAY

Dear God, please help me not put things off so I can get things done and have fun, too! Amen.

Nothing is Too Hard for God

"God can do anything!"

Luke 1:37 NCV

Have you ever had a problem that you thought was too big to fix? If you haven't yet, someday you probably will. The good news is that God can do the impossible!

The Bible is full of stories about God doing things that people said couldn't be done. David and Goliath. Moses and the Red Sea. Gideon and the Midianites. Joshua and the city of Jericho.

No matter what you face, God is strong enough to take care of it. Nothing is too hard for Him!

THOUGHT OF THE DAY

Can you name three heroes from the Bible who did the impossible with God?

PRAY TODAY

Dear God, nothing is impossible for You! So whenever I face an impossible problem, I will ask You for help. Amen.

THINK ABOUT GOOD THINGS

Fix your thoughts on what is true and good and right. Think about things that are pure and lovely, and dwell on the fine, good things in others. Think about all you can praise God for and be glad about.

Philippians 4:8 TLB

Did you know you can choose what you think about? And whether you think about good things or not-so-good things can make a big difference in your life! Why? Because what you think about often determines who you become and what you do.

That is why the Bible tells us to "fix our thoughts" on what is good and right and true. Choose wisely–what you think about matters!

THOUGHT OF THE DAY
Find good things to think about today!

PRAY TODAY
Dear God, I will choose to think on good things today. Amen.

iT Pays To Be Patient

Let your patience show itself perfectly in what you do.

James 1:4 NCV

Sometimes, it's hard to be patient, especially if you want something very badly. Waiting can seem like an eternity! But patience always pays off.

Abraham learned this lesson when God promised him that he would have a son. Abraham dreamed and waited, but it took twenty-five years from the time God made that promise until Isaac was born.

Twenty-five years is a long time to wait for something, but Abraham wasn't sorry for any of it. You won't be either!

THOUGHT OF THE DAY

Patience pays off. Trust God to let things happen at the right time.

PRAY TODAY

Dear God, being patient is really, really, really hard sometimes. Thank You for helping me. Amen.

WHAT WOULD JESUS DO?

Be imitators of God, therefore, as dearly loved children.

Ephesians 5:1 NIV

Do you ever wonder what the right thing is to do? Life can be confusing sometimes. Your friends might tell you one thing; your parents another. You might see something else on TV that makes you wonder what is really right and what is wrong.

That's why God wants you to study the Bible and the stories about Jesus. Learn about His life, and what He said and did, then you can follow His example.

The next time you aren't sure what to do, ask yourself, What would Jesus do? Then do it!

THOUGHT OF THE DAY

Can you think of something that Jesus did that surprised you?

PRAY TODAY

Dear God, please always show me the right thing to do. I want to be like Jesus. Amen.

Watching Over You

The Lord watches over you—the Lord is your shade at your right hand; the sun will not harm you by day, nor the moon by night.

Psalm 121:5-6 NIV

Even when nobody else is watching, God is. The Bible says He never sleeps. Which is a good thing, because that means when we are asleep, or not paying attention, God is always there looking out for us.

When you go to bed tonight, think about how wonderful it is that God loves you so much that you are never out of His sight or not in His thoughts. That means you can talk to Him at any time, too. He is always ready to listen!

THOUGHT OF THE DAY

God is watching out for you even while you are sleeping! Isn't that amazing?

PRAY TODAY

Dear God, I know that You are everywhere and that You are always with me. Thank You for watching over me. Amen.

JUST DO IT!

Everyone then who hears these words of mine and does them will be like a wise man who built his house on the rock.

Matthew 7:24 ESV

How can you show God how much you love Him? By doing your best to "do" what the Bible says!

You can "hear" what God says when you go to church, or read the Bible, or listen to your parents share about God. But God doesn't want you to just hear–He wants you to do it!

When you do your best to live like God wants you to, you show Him that you have real respect for Him. So put everything you've learned into action today!

THOUGHT OF THE DAY

What are three ways you can be a "doer" of the Word?

PRAY TODAY

Dear God, I really do love You. Please help me to do what You want me to. Amen.

Say You're Sorry

Therefore, confess your sins to one another and pray for one another, that you may be healed.

James 5:16 ESV

When you make a mistake or hurt someone's feelings, what should you do? The most important thing is to say you're sorry and ask for forgiveness, as soon as you can.

Many times, the longer you wait to apologize, the harder it becomes. But admitting you were wrong and asking for forgiveness is a powerful thing–it can sometimes even help bring you closer to the person you have hurt!

So if know you have done something wrong, don't be afraid to ask for forgiveness . . . right away!

THOUGHT OF THE DAY

If you don't know what to say, just try two words: "I'm sorry."

PRAY TODAY

Dear God, when I make a mistake, help me be quick to admit it, and quick to ask for forgiveness.
Amen.

in His Footsteps

For you were called to this, because Christ also suffered for you, leaving you an example, so that you should follow in His steps.

1 Peter 2:21 HCSB

Did you know that Jesus has left "footprints" for you to follow? No, there aren't real footprints all over the ground. It means that Jesus showed you how to live. That's what "following Him" is all about.

What did Jesus do? Was he kind? Did he tell the truth? Did he spend time with God? Once you see the footprint, then follow. . . .

THOUGHT OF THE DAY

Always ask yourself, "What would Jesus do?" Ask God to help you follow His footprints!

PRAY TODAY

Dear God, today and every day I want to follow Jesus. Help me do what He would do now and always. Amen.

Loud and Clear

Here's what you do: Live well, live wisely, live humbly. It's the way you live, not the way you talk, that counts.

James 3:13 MSG

Have you ever noticed that there are some people who talk a lot? They might go on and on about themselves and how great they are. But the Bible says that how we live is much more important than what we say. In other words, it's what you do that counts.

Being a good example so others will want to know Jesus is important. But don't worry about saying it—just focus on doing it by making good choices that would make God happy. People will "hear" you loud and clear!

THOUGHT OF THE DAY

Let your actions do all the talking.

PRAY TODAY

Dear God, help me remember to let my actions do the talking, instead of just my words. I want to please You. Amen.

Faith is . . .

Now faith is the reality of what is hoped for, the proof of what is not seen.

Hebrews 11:1 HCSB

How do we know God is real? For many people, it can be hard to believe in something that we can't see or touch. That's where faith comes in.

Faith is believing in something that you can't see . . . trusting in your heart that God is real. You may not realize it, but God has placed a seed of faith in your heart.

Believe in God and accept His love for you. If you believe that He is real and that He loves you, then you will know what God's love feels like. There is nothing that can compare to it!

THOUGHT OF THE DAY

Wish you could see God? Just close your eyes and imagine that you are snuggled in His lap. He will take care of you.

PRAY TODAY

Dear God, thank You for giving me faith. Please help it grow so I can always know Your love. Amen.

DON'T GET TANGLED UP

Trouble pursues the sinner, but the righteous are rewarded with good things.

Proverbs 13:21 NIV

Have you ever wondered why some kids just seem to make trouble all the time? Maybe they want attention or think their behavior is funny. But one thing is for sure . . . that type of behavior only gets more dangerous as you get older.

You are smarter than that! Don't get tangled up in trouble—instead, look for ways to avoid it. Make friends with people who want to do what's right. Make good choices. Don't give in to temptation. You'll be happier and God will reward you with good things.

THOUGHT OF THE DAY

If you aren't sure if something is a good idea, ask yourself what your parents would say.

PRAY TODAY

Dear God, thank You for giving me good friends and helping me make good choices so I can stay out of trouble. Amen.

WILLING TO FORGIVE

You must make allowance for each other's faults and forgive the person who offends you. Remember, the Lord forgave you, so you must forgive others.

Colossians 3:13 NLT

The Bible tells us that when people do things that are wrong, we should forgive them. That can be a hard thing to do sometimes. The good news is that God is quick to forgive us for the mistakes we make, and remembering that helps us to forgive others.

Has somebody done something that hurt your feelings or made you angry? If you need to, talk things over with your mom or dad, and then be ready to forgive the person who upset you. If you are willing to try, God will help you do it!

THOUGHT OF THE DAY

The next time you need to forgive, think about the last time you needed forgiveness.

PRAY TODAY

Dear God, when I have trouble forgiving someone, help me remember how much You love me and how many times You have forgiven me. Amen.

a Powerful Life

God's Way is not a matter of mere talk; it's an empowered life.

1 Corinthians 4:20 MSG

What is an "empowered life"? It is living a life that is doing your best, being your best, and trusting God when bad things happen. And sometimes they do. But the great news is that with God you will be able to live "powerfully." He will make you brave and strong. He will help you with your problems. And God will even help you find ways to help others. With God, you can do amazing things and He wants to give you the power to do them!

THOUGHT OF THE DAY

Always remember that with God, you are loved!

PRAY TODAY

Dear God, I want to do things Your way so I can live my life the best way possible. Thank You for helping me. Amen.

WHAT KIND OF TREE ARE YOU?

For every tree is known by its own fruit.

Luke 6:44 NKJV

Have you ever seen apples growing on an orange tree? Of course not–that's just silly!

Jesus explained that we will either produce "good fruit" or "bad fruit," depending on what is in our hearts.

What kind of good fruit are we talking about? Things like love, joy, peace, patience, kindness, goodness, faithfulness, gentleness, and self-control. That means if we know and love God, we will grow good fruit in our lives and people will be able to see that we belong to Him. What kind of tree do you want to be?

THOUGHT OF THE DAY

What kind of fruit do others see in your life?

PRAY TODAY

Dear God, thank You for helping me grow lots of good fruit in my life. Amen.

Do it God's Way!

We must obey God rather than any human authority.

Acts 5:29 NLT

In the story of Joshua and the city of Jericho, the children of Israel finally got to go into the Promised Land. Boy, were they excited!

But, when God told them what He wanted them to do, suddenly everyone had a better idea than God. In fact, they seemed to forget all the miracles God had already done for them.

Fortunately, Joshua convinced everyone to do things God's way. They marched around Jericho seven times, blew the trumpets and shouted, and the walls fell down! Then they were really glad they did it God's way!

THOUGHT OF THE DAY

Obeying is really all about trust.

PRAY TODAY

Dear God, sometimes I have good ideas, but I know Yours are always better. Help me follow Your instructions. Amen.

Be a Friend!

Greater love has no one than this, that someone lay down his life for his friends.

John 15:13 ESV

Laura and Junior have been friends for a long time. They know that friendship can be a wonderful thing. The very best friends always have your back and stick with you no matter what happens.

That's why it's good to know how to make and to keep good friends. How do you do it? Remember to treat people the way you want to be treated. Be kind. Share. Say nice things. Be helpful. Pay attention to how they feel. When you do, you'll see that making friends isn't hard at all!

THOUGHT OF THE DAY

What makes your friends happy? Pick two kind things to do for them this week.

PRAY TODAY

Dear God, help me be a good friend to others and do whatever I can to help them. Amen.

Kindness Starts with You

Be kind to one another, tender-hearted, forgiving each other, just as God in Christ also has forgiven you.

Ephesians 4:32 NASB

If you're waiting for other people to be nice to you before you're nice to them, you've got it backwards. Kindness starts with you!

You see, you can never control what other people will say or do, but you can control your own choices. And the Bible tells us that we should never stop being kind, no matter how others treat us.

Today, look for a chance to do something nice for someone. They might not be kind to you, but you might make a new friend. You'll never know unless you try!

THOUGHT OF THE DAY

Is there someone at school who you think doesn't like you? Try doing something nice for them. They just might surprise you!

PRAY TODAY

Dear God, help me be kind to others, even when it's hard. Amen.

DOING THE RIGHT THING

He grants a treasure of common sense to the honest. He is a shield to those who walk with integrity.

Proverbs 2:7 NLT

When you choose to do the right thing, you never have to worry about what you did or what you said. If you always tell the truth, you never have to worry about getting caught in a lie. And God promises He will shield and protect you.

It's just common sense—if you do something that you know is wrong, you'll be worried that someone will find out.

But God loves it when you make the choice to do the right thing. It may be harder in the beginning, but it's always better—and safer—in the end.

THOUGHT OF THE DAY

You can't go wrong if you do the right thing!

PRAY TODAY

Dear God, sometimes it's hard to make the right choice. But even when doing the right thing is hard, I know You will help me. Amen.

The Golden Rule

Therefore, whatever you want others to do for you, do also the same for them—this is the Law and the Prophets.

Matthew 7:12 HCSB

The words of Matthew 7:12 are often called the "Golden Rule." Jesus taught that this one rule sums up a whole lot of rules about how we should treat each other.

So, what does the Golden Rule mean? Would you want people to treat you kindly? Tell you the truth? Forgive you if you make a mistake? Show you respect? Of course! Always keep that in mind, and you will be "golden."

THOUGHT OF THE DAY

The secret to following the Golden Rule is to always put yourself in the other person's shoes.

PRAY TODAY

Dear God, thank You for helping me remember to always treat others the way I want to be treated. Amen.

Never Stop Growing

So that you may walk worthy of the Lord, fully pleasing to Him, bearing fruit in every good work and growing in the knowledge of God.

Colossians 1:10 HCSB

Every day, you're learning new things and doing new things. You're growing up and that's exciting! But do you sometimes wish you were older than you are? Maybe all grown up and on your own?

Most kids feel this way at one time or another, but you might be surprised to learn that no matter how old you get, you'll never be done growing! Even adults need to keep growing in faith, wisdom, and love.

So don't be in a hurry . . . just do your best to follow God. There are many wonderful things ahead!

THOUGHT OF THE DAY

Grownups still have plenty to learn . . . and so do you!

PRAY TODAY

Dear God, help me grow a little bit more every day so I can become the person You want me to be. Amen.

a Positive Change

You put on the new self, the one created according to God's likeness in righteousness and purity of the truth.

Ephesians 4:24 HCSB

Do you have some habits you wish you could break? Perhaps you've tried to change or make better choices, but you're still falling back into your old habits. If so, don't get discouraged. Instead, keep trying to be the person God wants you to be.

Even a small positive change can make a big difference. And if you trust God and keep asking for His help to change your bad habits, He will help you do it. So, make a step in the right direction and keep praying. You can do it!

THOUGHT OF THE DAY

Today, make one good choice. It can change everything!

PRAY TODAY

Dear God, help me not give up when things get hard. I want to make You happy and do what's right. Amen.

Take a Time Out

Truly my soul silently waits for God; from Him comes my salvation.

Psalm 62:1 NKJV

The Bible tells us that we should "Be still before the Lord and wait patiently for Him" (Psalm 37:7 NIV). But most of the time it's really hard to be still, and sometimes it's even harder to be patient! But don't worry, you can do it.

Sometimes we get so busy that we miss out on what God wants to tell us. That's when we need to take a little "time out" with God, to be still and wait on Him. If you do, He won't disappoint you. He wants to be with you even more than you want to be with Him!

THOUGHT OF THE DAY

Take five minutes today and get quiet and still. You might be surprised by what you hear!

PRAY TODAY

Dear God, help me to remember to take a break and spend time with You. I want to hear everything You have to tell me! Amen.

Don't Judge!

"Don't criticize, and then you won't be criticized. For others will treat you as you treat them."

Matthew 7:1-2 TLB

The Bible says if you judge other people in a mean or critical way, the same thing will happen to you. And that is not a very fun experience!

Don't be tempted to blame, criticize, or pick on people for things like the way they look, the stuff they don't have, where they live, or the things they do wrong. God wants you to show love to people–even if they aren't perfect. And that's a really good thing, because nobody's perfect!

THOUGHT OF THE DAY

It's easy to find things wrong in other people. Instead, take the time to look for something good.

PRAY TODAY

Dear God, help me to not judge people and to always be kind. Amen.

Take a Minute

So through Jesus let us always offer to God our sacrifice of praise, coming from lips that speak his name.

Hebrews 13:15 NCV

Everything you have–family, friends, toys, clothes, food–comes from God. He loves you so much and goes out of His way to make sure you are blessed. Today, take a minute to thank God for His blessings and for His love, and just praise Him for being God!

Praise can happen lots of ways. Saying "thank you," singing a special song, telling others about how awesome God is. Throughout your day, look for chances to give Him praise.

THOUGHT OF THE DAY

Sing your favorite song from church with all your heart!

PRAY TODAY

Dear God, I praise You for everything You've done for me. Thank You for loving me and taking care of me. Amen.

Listen for Wisdom

My child, listen to what I say and remember what I command you. Listen carefully to wisdom; set your mind on understanding.

Proverbs 2:1-2 NCV

Do you sit quietly when your parents and your teachers are talking? Have you learned how to listen respectfully–with a quiet, attentive spirit and your ears open wide? If so, you have mastered a great skill!

Listening is important for many things, but it is the very best way to learn wisdom. There is a lot you can learn from the people in your life, but you might miss it if you aren't paying attention and listening carefully. It isn't always easy, but keep practicing!

THOUGHT OF THE DAY

Listening doesn't come easily to most people. Just don't give up!

PRAY TODAY

Dear God, make me a good listener, especially when I need to learn wisdom. Amen.

Just Celebrate!

Celebrate God all day, every day. I mean, revel in him!

Philippians 4:4 MSG

D o you expect God to do wonderful things for you to-day? Sometimes we forget that God is on our side and is the one who is responsible for all the good things in our lives.

Can you think of something special that has hap-poned to you lately? Are you happy about your family, your friends, and your church? Hopefully so!

After all, God loves you, and that fact should make you very happy indeed. So think about how good God is today–and celebrate Him!

THOUGHT OF THE DAY

Heaven is going to be one big party–but we can start celebrating now!

PRAY TODAY

Dear God, help me remember that every day is day to celebrate! Amen.

You Can't Please Everybody

My son, if sinners entice you, don't be persuaded.

Proverbs 1:10 HCSB

Here's an important lesson to remember: you can't please everybody. If you try to make your friends like you by doing things you know you shouldn't-watch out!

It's much more important to focus on pleasing God. He always wants what is best for you, but "friends" who tempt you to do things that are wrong are not looking out for you.

The only way to avoid bad consequences is to make good choices-even if you are the only one. Don't worry about everybody else . . . just please God!

THOUGHT OF THE DAY

Don't worry about impressing others-either they already like you or they don't.

PRAY TODAY

Dear God, pleasing people is not nearly as important as pleasing You. Help me make good choices. Amen.

Be Nice to Your Family

If a kingdom is divided against itself, that kingdom cannot stand. If a house is divided against itself, that house will not be able to stand.

Mark 3:24-25 NASB

What is a divided house? A family that doesn't stick together and work as a team, especially when things go wrong.

God made families because we all need a safe place that feels like home, where we are loved for who we are. We all need to feel like we belong and that someone will stick by us, no matter what.

If your family has a hard time sticking together, ask God to show you how to help change that. And if you have a great team at home, thank Him for the wonderful family you have!

THOUGHT OF THE DAY

Every family gets on each other's nerves sometimes. When that happens, don't say words that are unkind. Instead, take a break!

PRAY TODAY

Dear God, thank You for my family. Help me always remember to treat them with love and respect. Amen.

God's Promise

I assure you: Anyone who believes has eternal life.

John 6:47 HCSB

God made a promise a long time ago—He sent His Son Jesus to save the world and to save you! No one has ever made a promise bigger than that.

What does it mean to know Jesus? No matter where you are, God is with you. No matter what happens or what you do, God loves you. No matter what choices you make, God never gives up on you.

Most importantly, God sent His Son so that you can live forever in heaven. Wow! Now that's the best gift ever.

THOUGHT OF THE DAY

God always keeps His promises!

PRAY TODAY

Dear God, thank You for all of Your promises to me, and that we will always be together. Amen.

He is everywhere

God did this so that men would seek him and perhaps reach out for him and find him, though he is not far from each one of us.

Acts 17:27 NIV

God is everywhere you have ever been and everywhere you will ever go. That's why you can speak to God any time you need to.

If you are afraid or discouraged, you can turn to God for strength. If you are worried, you can trust God's promises. If you are happy, you can thank Him for His gifts. And if you are excited, you can tell Him whatever great thing has happened.

God is right here with you, ready and waiting to listen. He always wants to hear from you, so why not talk to Him now?

THOUGHT OF THE DAY

You are never far away from God. If you are in trouble, ask Him for help.

PRAY TODAY

Dear God, thank You that You never leave me, and You are always listening to my thoughts and to my prayers. Amen.

NOBODY'S PERFECT

If we confess our sins to him, he is faithful and just to forgive us and to cleanse us from every wrong.

1 John 1:9 NLT

When you make a mistake, do you get really mad at yourself . . . or maybe really, really, really mad? Hopefully not! After all, everybody makes mistakes, and nobody's perfect!

Even when you make mistakes, God loves you and forgives you . . . so you should love and forgive yourself, too.

The next time you make a mistake, learn from it. But don't be too hard on yourself. God doesn't expect you to be perfect!

THOUGHT OF THE DAY

A mistake is something you can always learn from and do better next time.

PRAY TODAY

Dear God, when I make mistakes, help me to admit it and apologize if I need to. Thank You for Your forgiveness and for Your love. Amen.

Share Your Stuff

"It is more blessed to give than to receive."

Acts 20:35 HCSB

Do you have a closet filled up with too much stuff? If so, it might be a good time to share some of it.

Think about all the kids who could enjoy the things that you don't use very much. Maybe you've outgrown some clothes, or have stopped playing with some of your toys. There are always people who need help and it makes God happy when we give to others.

Talk to your parents about some ways that you can give–it can really be a lot of fun. Even better than Christmas morning!

THOUGHT OF THE DAY

Giving will always make you feel better than receiving.

PRAY TODAY

Dear God, You have given me so many things–more than I really need. Help me to give freely. Amen.

Tell it Like it is

I have no greater joy than this: to hear that my children are walking in the truth.

3 John 1:4 HCSB

Have you ever told a fib to try and get out of trouble? If so, you probably know that fibs can quickly get out of control. In fact, you might have to keep telling lie after lie, just to keep from getting caught and the truth from coming out!

But the Bible says that God loves it when we "walk in truth." It is always best to be completely honest. Even if you think you are going to get in trouble, it is better to face the consequences for your mistake rather than make it worse by lying.

The best thing to do is to always tell it like it is!

THOUGHT OF THE DAY

Truth is always your friend.

PRAY TODAY

Dear God, help me not give in to the temptation to exaggerate, fib, or lie my way out of a problem. The truth is always best. Amen.

Time for God

Be gracious to me, Lord, for I call to You all day long.

Psalm 86:3 HCSB

Guess what? God is really glad that you are taking the time to read this book! Whether you find a few minutes when you get up, at lunchtime, or before you go to bed at night, God loves spending time with you!

Grownups call these times "devotions," which really just means that you make some time to focus all of your energy and attention on God. It is during those times that your relationship with God grows stronger. It can be the very best part of your day!

THOUGHT OF THE DAY

What are some new things you have learned about God since you have been reading this book?

PRAY TODAY

Dear God, I love to talk to You every day. Thank You for always being there for me. Amen.

Friends Who Make You Better

As iron sharpens iron, so people can improve each other.

Proverbs 27:17 NCV

Are your friends the kind of kids who encourage you to do what's right? If so, you've chosen your friends wisely. But if your friends tend to get in trouble a lot, perhaps it's time to think about making some new ones.

Whether you know it or not, you're probably going to act a lot like your friends do. That can either be a good thing, or a not-so-good thing. So choose friends who make you want to be your very best self. You can do the same thing for them, too!

THOUGHT OF THE DAY

Watch and listen carefully before you decide to be good friends with someone.

PRAY TODAY

Dear God, help me choose my friends carefully, so we can help each other be what You want us to be. Amen.

Practice Love

Dear friends, let us practice loving each other, for love comes from God and those who are loving and kind show that they are the children of God, and that they are getting to know him better. But if a person isn't loving and kind, it shows that he doesn't know God–for God is love.

1 John 4:7-8 TLB

Sometimes, people can say hurtful things without thinking–it's easy to make that mistake sometimes. But some people can be mean and cruel on purpose. That's called being a bully, and that behavior is wrong. Always!

If you see other kids saying unkind things or making fun of someone, you should ask them to stop. God wants us to show love and kindness to everyone–no matter who they are! So stand up for anyone who needs your help, and practice love and kindness today.

THOUGHT OF THE DAY

Always do what's right! Stand up for the people who need your help.

PRAY TODAY

Dear God, if other people are being mean, give me courage to do what's right. Amen.

Getting to Know Him

Jesus said to him, "I am the way, and the truth, and the life. No one comes to the Father except through me."

John 14:6 ESV

There's really no way around it: If you want to know God, you need to know His Son. And that's good, because getting to know Jesus is a wonderful thing!

Jesus has an amazing love for you. Not only did He die for you, but because He came to Earth to live just like us, He understands every problem and temptation you face.

Jesus desperately wants to introduce you to His Father and show you the life He has planned for you. So welcome Him into your heart today. You will be so glad you did!

THOUGHT OF THE DAY

What is your favorite story from the Bible about Jesus?

PRAY TODAY

Dear God, thank You for Jesus. He is my friend, and I want to know Him better every day. Amen.

Keep it Up!

So don't get tired of doing what is good. Don't get discouraged and give up, for we will reap a harvest of blessing at the appropriate time.

Galatians 6:9 NLT

The Bible teaches us to treat other people with respect, kindness, courtesy, and love. You might wonder sometimes if anybody notices when you do these things, or if it really ever makes a difference. Well, it does!

The Bible says we shouldn't get tired of doing the right thing. That if we keep treating others the way we are supposed to, that God will reward us when the time is right. God always sees your efforts, and He is pleased and proud of you. So don't quit . . . keep it up!

THOUGHT OF THE DAY
Doing the right thing always makes you feel great.

PRAY TODAY
Dear God, please help me to keep doing what You want me to do. I won't give up. Amen.

a Party That never ends

A cheerful heart has a continual feast.

Proverbs 15:15 HCSB

What is a continual feast? It's a little bit like a non-stop birthday party: fun, fun, and more fun! The Bible tells us that a cheerful heart can make life like a never-ending party.

Where does cheerfulness begin? It begins inside of you–in your heart. A cheerful heart is a choice, not the result of how things are going.

That's a good thing! That means you can have a cheerful heart by being thankful, thoughtful, kind, and joyful. Let the party begin!

THOUGHT OF THE DAY

A cheerful heart is a wonderful thing to share with family and friends!

PRAY TODAY

Dear God, I want Your love and joy to live in my heart today and forever. Amen.

SHARING IS BETTER

And God will generously provide all you need. Then you will always have everything you need and plenty left over to share with others.

2 Corinthians 9:8 NLT

God promises to give us everything we need, but sometimes, all we can think about is what we want that we don't have. Madame Blueberry had this problem, but she quickly learned that getting more and more stuff only left her sad and lonely.

Stuff can't make you feel better, but sharing and giving can! Don't worry about yourself–God will take care of you! Instead, look for ways to share what you have. Sharing is so much better!

THOUGHT OF THE DAY

When you give what you can to others, you'll get a lot of joy in return!

PRAY TODAY

Dear God, help me to share with those who need my help today. Amen.

LOVING CORRECTION

But don't, dear friend, resent God's discipline; don't sulk under his loving correction. It's the child he loves that God corrects; a father's delight is behind all this.

Proverbs 3:11-12 MSG

The Bible says that when people make mistakes, God corrects them. And that means that if you make a mistake, God will find a way to teach you what you need to know to avoid doing the same thing again.

Don't worry, God doesn't expect you to be perfect. He just wants you to be able to learn from your mistakes. And He always wants the best for you because He loves you, just like your parents do.

Trust Him! God wants to see you become the person He created you to be.

THOUGHT OF THE DAY

When you make a mistake, ask your parents for advice. You might be surprised by what they say!

PRAY TODAY

Dear God, sometimes I make mistakes, and when I do, please help me learn from them. Amen.

How Will They Know?

"This is how everyone will recognize that you are my disciples—when they see the love you have for each other."

John 13:35 MSG

How do people know that you love God? Well, you can tell them, of course. And talking about your faith in God is a very good thing to do. But Jesus said people would be able to tell that you follow Him by doing one simple thing—loving others.

Sometimes, loving people isn't easy. But choosing to love someone even when it's hard is exactly the moment when God shines the brightest in you.

Today, look for ways to show God's love to the people you meet. They'll know something is different about you!

THOUGHT OF THE DAY

Write down three things you can do for someone you know who is really hard to love!

PRAY TODAY

Dear God, I want people to be able to tell that I know You. Help me show love to others all the time. Amen.

Keep Believing

Immediately the father of the child cried out and said with tears, "Lord, I believe; help my unbelief!"

Mark 9:24 NKJV

Are you the type of kid who has lots and lots of questions? Do most of them start with "Why . . . ?" If so, you'll be glad to know that you can ask God anything and everything!

God has all kinds of answers for you—and you can find many of them in the Bible. Sometimes though, the answers don't come right away, and things can be hard to understand.

But in those moments, trust in God and keep believing. God won't let you down.

THOUGHT OF THE DAY
Trust in God, no matter what.

PRAY TODAY
Dear God, I know that I can't understand everything that happens. But I trust You. Help me stay strong. Amen.

You are Special

To acquire wisdom is to love oneself; people who cherish understanding will prosper.

Proverbs 19:8 NLT

The only person in the world who is exactly like you . . . is you! That's pretty amazing if you think about it.

Larry learned that he didn't have to be a super-hero to be special to God. And that meant that by loving himself, he could help people and do really big, superhero things.

The same goes for you. You may not be LarryBoy, but you are a V.I.P. What is that? A "Very Important Person," of course!

THOUGHT OF THE DAY

Love yourself because God loves you, which is the love that matters most!

PRAY TODAY

Dear God, I know that there is only one me in the whole world. Thanks for making me special. Amen.

iT'S GooD To Have GooD FRienDS

My dear, dear friends, if God loved us like this, we certainly ought to love each other.

1 John 4:11 MSG

One of the best gifts God will ever give you is a good, kind friend. Do you have some good and kind friends in your life? How do they help you? What do you do to help them?

Be thankful today for the good friends you have. And show them how much you appreciate them by being a good friend to them, too.

THOUGHT OF THE DAY

Never forget to thank God for your friends!

PRAY TODAY

Dear God, thank You for my friends, and help me be the best friend I can be. Amen.

Ready and Waiting

Rejoice always! Pray constantly. Give thanks in everything, for this is God's will for you in Christ Jesus.

1 Thessalonians 5:16-18 HCSB

Some people wonder what it is God wants them to do. That's called "knowing God's will." One thing's for sure, God's will for all of us is to rejoice always, pray about everything, and give thanks in everything!

So, no matter what is going on in your life, if you talk to God from your heart, He is always there to listen and help. God wants to guide you through the hard times and rejoice with you in the great ones.

So don't worry about things; pray about them. You'll discover that God is always near and ready to listen.

THOUGHT OF THE DAY

God is always listening and understands your heart, even when you can't find the right words.

PRAY TODAY

Dear God, thank You for always being there for me and for all the wonderful things You do. Amen.

Happy Thoughts

Those who are pure in their thinking are happy, because they will be with God.

Matthew 5:8 NCV

Have you ever heard the expression, "You are what you eat"? Well, the same is true for what you think! The Bible talks a lot about our thoughts, and says that we should think about things that are good and pure and lovely. God doesn't want you to spend your time thinking about sad, gloomy, or bad things. He wants you to think happy thoughts, like about how much He loves you; your family; your friends; your favorite things to do.

Think on good and pure things. It will do you good!

THOUGHT OF THE DAY

Focus on one happy thought, and see how it changes your attitude today!

PRAY TODAY

Dear God, help me think about good things today. Like how much You love me. Amen.

How to Treat Others

For if you refuse to act kindly, you can hardly expect to be treated kindly. Kind mercy wins over harsh judgment every time.

James 2:12-13 MSG

We all like to be treated with kindness—even a warm smile can make the day feel happier. The trick is to pay attention to how you treat others. If you are kind and thoughtful, treat people with respect, and forgive when they make a mistake, you can be sure your kindness will come back to you.

THOUGHT OF THE DAY

Before you say or do anything, make sure it is full of kindness.

PRAY TODAY

Dear God, I want to be helpful and kind. Please show me the best way to treat others. Amen.

PRAY FOR EVERYBODY

Love your enemies. Pray for those who hurt you.

Matthew 5:44 NCV

It's usually pretty easy to pray for your friends and family, because those are the people you love most. But when it comes to praying for people who have hurt you, well that's a different thing entirely!

The Bible tells us that God wants us to pray for the folks we don't like, too. Why? God wants you to do it because he knows it's really the best thing for you. And your prayers might just make a big difference for them, too!

THOUGHT OF THE DAY

What's the secret to forgiving others? Remember all the things God has forgiven you for.

PRAY TODAY

Dear God, I know forgiving others is important to You. So please give me a forgiving heart, Lord. Amen.

You Make a Difference

For the Son of man shall come in the glory of his Father with his angels; and then he shall reward every man according to his works.

Matthew 16:27 KJV

Do you wonder if the good things you do for others really matter that much? Well, they do!

Even if it occms that other people don't notice or appreciate what you are doing, God does! Nothing you do escapes His notice. And sometimes, you might not realize how much people are touched by your thoughtfulness. Even the smallest acts of kindness can make a big difference!

So just keep doing your best, and trust God. He is proud of you!

THOUGHT OF THE DAY

What's an easy way to change someone's day? Smile!

PRAY TODAY

Dear God, help me to always do good things to help people. Amen.

WHO YOU BELONG TO

Tell each other the truth because we all belong to each other.

Ephesians 4:25 ICB

It's important to be honest. When you tell the truth, you'll feel better about yourself, and other people will feel better about you, too.

God says we belong to each other–like a family. And truthfulness is really important to keep a family healthy and happy.

It's always better to be honest, even when it's hard. So, when you are tempted to lie, just remember what God said about lying and always tell the truth!

THOUGHT OF THE DAY
Telling the truth is always the best way to go!

PRAY TODAY
Dear God, help me to always tell the truth. I want to honor You and others every day of my life. Amen.

Honor God

"You shall have no other gods before me."

Exodus 20:3 ESV

God gave the Ten Commandments to Moses. These were the laws that God wanted His people to follow so they could be safe and happy.

The first three commandments talk about the most important thing of all: having a relationship with God.

What are those first three commandments? First, love God more than anything else. Second, make God the most important thing in your life. And third, always say God's name with love and respect. Wonderful rules to live by!

THOUGHT OF THE DAY

Make God the most important part of your life!

PRAY TODAY

Dear God, please help me to put You first. I want to love You, honor You, and always show You respect. Amen.

Time with God

But when you pray, go into your private room, shut your door, and pray to your Father who is in secret.

Matthew 6:6 HCSB

It's always great to spend time with God at church or with your family, but it's also really great to spend time with Him all by yourself . . . just you and Him! Talking to Him, letting Him know what's going on with you and how you feel, and reading the Bible–all these things help you know Him better!

Just like your family and friends, your relationship with God needs time. Time for talking, listening, and just being together. So make some time in your day for Him . . . every day. You will be glad you did!

THOUGHT OF THE DAY

Get up 30 minutes earlier in the morning and spend that time with God!

PRAY TODAY

Dear God, I have lots of things to do, but I don't want to be too busy for you. Help me find time to spend with You every day. Amen.

a Light of Kindness

Let everyone see that you are gentle and kind. The Lord is coming soon.

Philippians 4:5 NCV

The Bible tells us that Jesus is coming back soon! Until He comes, God wants us to be gentle and kind to everyone.

Showing kindness to others is an important job! People need to know how much God loves them and that He can help them when they are in trouble. And they learn about God's love by watching you. So keep it up—your light is shining!

THOUGHT OF THE DAY

Think of someone you can show kindness to today.

PRAY TODAY

Dear God, help me shine Your light in the darkness and show people how much You love them. Amen.

STUFF, STUFF, and MORE STUFF

Seek first God's kingdom and what God wants. Then all your other needs will be met as well.

Matthew 6:33 NCV

Many people spend all their time thinking about stuff-buying stuff, getting stuff, having stuff. Needing better stuff than someone else's stuff. Wanting the newest and coolest stuff.

Don't let that happen to you! God said that if we seek Him first and do what He wants us to, He will give us everything we need.

That's pretty amazing. And the best part is you won't make yourself crazy over all that stuff! So decide to seek God today.

THOUGHT OF THE DAY

What's one way you can seek God today?

PRAY TODAY

Dear God, help me stop worrying about stuff and instead pay attention to what matters to You. Amen.

EVERYBODY MAKES MISTAKES

No one in this world always does right.

Ecclesiastes 7:20 CEV

D o you make mistakes? Of course you do . . . everybody does. When you make a mistake, the important thing is to try your best to learn from it so that you won't make the very same mistake again. And, if you have hurt someone or disappointed God or someone close to you, you should ask for forgiveness.

Remember: mistakes are a part of life. Some mistakes are bigger than others, but no one can say they always do the right thing. So don't worry! Just keep trying to do better next time.

THOUGHT OF THE DAY

If you make a mistake, don't try to deny it! Just admit it and move on.

PRAY TODAY

Dear God, help me learn from my mistakes so that I can be a better person. Amen.

Living The Good Life

I have chosen the way of faithfulness; I set your rules before me.

Psalm 119:30 ESV

God has rules for living, and He really wants you to obey them. He wants you to be fair, honest, and kind. He wants you to behave well, and He wants you to respect your parents.

Why does God want you do all these things? Well, it's because He wants you to live a life that is happy and blessed . . . and He wants you to honor Him with how you live and the choices you make. That way people will see God's love when they see you!

THOUGHT OF THE DAY

God wants you to do the right things because it's the best thing for you!

PRAY TODAY

Dear God, please help me pay attention to the rules that You want me to follow so my life can be the best it can be. Amen.

Heavenly Peace

I leave you peace. My peace I give you. I do not give it to you as the world does. So don't let your hearts be troubled.

John 14:27 ICB

The Bible tells us that Jesus offers us peace, not like what the world gives, but a peace that is perfect. We can either accept His peace or ignore it.

When we accept the peace of Jesus Christ into our hearts, our lives are changed forever. Peace is God's gift to you; it is yours for the asking.

Ask Jesus for His peace. He is happy to give it to you!

THOUGHT OF THE DAY

You can handle anything if God's peace is in your heart!

PRAY TODAY

Dear God, I want to receive the special peace that You have to give me and then share it with others. Amen.

Keep Going!

Noah was another who trusted God. When he heard God's warning about the future, Noah believed him even though there was then no sign of a flood, and wasting no time, he built the ark and saved his family.

Hebrews 11:7 TLB

Do you remember the story of Noah? God told him to build a boat big enough to hold his family and every kind of animal, because a flood was coming that would destroy everything on the earth.

People thought he was crazy. They didn't believe what he said could happen. They made fun of Noah and ignored God's warning.

But what did Noah do? He believed God and built a boat. A huge boat. It took him a long time, but he kept going. And when the flood came, he was ready.

THOUGHT OF THE DAY

Do you think Noah wanted to give up? What made him keep going?

PRAY TODAY

Dear God, I want to believe You like Noah did. Please help me keep going, even when things seem impossible. Amen.

THE WAY, THE TRUTH, THE LIFE

Jesus answered, "I am the way and the truth and the life. No one comes to the Father except through me."

John 14:6 NIV

The Bible tells us that there is only one way to meet God–through His Son, Jesus.

Jesus is the Way, the Truth, and the Life. Because Jesus died for you, your sins are forgiven! So He makes the way for you to go to God yourself, without fear or worry. Through Jesus, you can know and love God, the Father, the way He has always wanted to know and love you.

Open your heart to Jesus today!

THOUGHT OF THE DAY

If Jesus says it's the truth–then it's the truth!

PRAY TODAY

Dear God, thank You for sending Jesus. I want to follow Him and know You more every day. Amen.

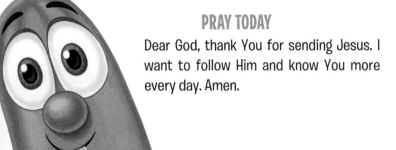

RESPECT FOR OTHERS

Being respected is more important than having great riches.

Proverbs 22:1 ICB

Bob knows that it is really important to try and have a respectful attitude towards others. What is respect? It is thinking and acting in a way that shows others you care about them and their feelings.

Should you be respectful of grown ups? Of course. Teachers? Certainly. Family members and friends? Yep, but it doesn't stop there. The Bible teaches us to treat all people with respect.

The more you show respect, the easier it becomes. So, start practicing right now! You'll be glad you did.

THOUGHT OF THE DAY
Jesus was always respectful of others.

PRAY TODAY
Dear God, I will try to show respect to everybody, starting with my family and my friends. Amen.

Telling the Truth

Don't ever forget kindness and truth. Wear them like a necklace. Write them on your heart as if on a tablet.

Proverbs 3:3 NCV

Sometimes when you want to remember something important you might write it down. Imagine if you hung that note around your neck, you'd probably remember it for sure!

God wants us to be sure and remember to be kind and truthful to everyone! And don't forget, happiness and honesty go hand in hand. The truth is always the best choice!

THOUGHT OF THE DAY

Another way to remember to be kind is to remember when someone was kind to you!

PRAY TODAY

Dear God, help me to always choose the truth and kindness, even when it's not easy to do. Amen.

He Answers

For I know the thoughts that I think toward you, says the Lord, thoughts of peace and not of evil, to give you a future and a hope. Then you will call upon Me and go and pray to Me, and I will listen to you.

Jeremiah 29:11-12 NKJV

Do you ever wonder if God really answers your prayers? The answer is yes! But the answer may come in a different way than you expect.

Sometimes, God may not answer your prayers as fast as you would like. Or the answer may not be what you think He will say. Many times, God says "yes," but sometimes, He says "no."

Fortunately, God has a plan and He's got everything under control. So keep praying, and when the time is right, He'll answer!

THOUGHT OF THE DAY

Don't worry about whether your words are the right words. Just talk to God from your heart.

PRAY TODAY

Dear God, thank You for always listening to my prayers. I know You will give me the answer I need. Amen.

Love Yourself, Too!

God began doing a good work in you, and I am sure he will continue it until it is finished when Jesus Christ comes again.

Philippians 1:6 NCV

The Bible says that you should love everybody–family, friends, and even your enemies! But it is easy to forget that the word "everybody" includes you.

Do you treat yourself with honor and respect? You should. After all, God created you In a very special way, and He loves you very much. And if God thinks you are amazing and wonderful, shouldn't you think about yourself in the same way? God wants you to learn to love yourself, too!

THOUGHT OF THE DAY

You are very special to God. What does the Bible say about who you are in Christ?

PRAY TODAY

Dear God, help me be kind to everybody, including myself. Help me to see myself the way You do. Amen.

Give God Your Worries

Give all your worries and cares to God, for he cares about what happens to you.

1 Peter 5:6 NLT

The Bible says we should give all our cares to God. He is more than able to handle any problem and He loves you so much that He is glad to do it.

What things are going on with you today? Whatever it is, God knows everything that is happening to you and He cares about every little detail. So why not let God take care of it?

THOUGHT OF THE DAY

Close your eyes and imagine handing God a box full of everything you care about.

PRAY TODAY

Dear God, I know You can handle anything that happens and that You care for me. Amen.

No Matter What

But your name shall be Abraham, for I have made you the father of a multitude of nations.

Genesis 17:5 ESV

Abraham was a man who loved God and believed what He said—no matter what. When God promised to make Abraham the "father of many nations," Abraham was already very old. Too old, many thought, for him to ever have one child—let alone enough to fill many nations!

But Abraham believed God. He knew that when God makes a promise, He always keeps it.

It took a little while, but just like God promised, Abraham had a son. And now, thousands of years later, his descendants are all around the world!

THOUGHT OF THE DAY
If God makes a promise, you can count on it!

PRAY TODAY
Dear God, I want to have faith like Abraham. Help me trust You no matter what. Amen.

an aTTiTuDe oF KinDness

Finally, all of you should be of one mind, full of sympathy toward each other, loving one another with tender hearts and humble minds.

1 Peter 3:8 NLT

A n attitude of kindness starts in your heart. Do you listen to your heart when it tells you to be kind to other people? That's always a good idea. After all, lots of people in the world aren't as fortunate as you are—and some of them are living very near you.

Ask your parents to help you find ways to do nice things for other people. And don't forget that everybody needs love, kindness, and respect. If you are always ready to share those things with others, you can make a difference wherever you go.

THOUGHT OF THE DAY

Try doing something kind for someone today. See how good it makes you feel.

PRAY TODAY

Dear God, You said that it's important to be kind. So I'll do my best to think of others and say and do things from a kind heart. Amen.

Making New Friends

When you're kind to others, you help yourself; when you're cruel to others, you hurt yourself.

Proverbs 11:17 MSG

D o you know the secret to making new friends? A wise old saying says it best: to have a friend you must first be a friend.

Simple, right? Simple, but not always easy. But you can do it!

Being a friend means doing things like letting others go first; offering to help someone who needs it; and making a point to show that you care. If you will remember that true friendship is about what you can give, not about what you get—you will always have plenty of wonderful friends!

THOUGHT OF THE DAY

Want to make a new friend? Learn about something that interests them.

PRAY TODAY

Dear God, I know it is better to give than to receive. So help me find ways I can bless my friends. Amen.

More Than You Can Count!

Then Peter came to him and asked, "Lord, how often should I forgive someone who sins against me? Seven times?" "No!" Jesus replied, "seventy times seven!"

Matthew 18:21-22 NLT

How often does God forgive us? More times than we can count! And that, by the way, is exactly how many times that God expects us to forgive other people—more times than we can count!

Forgiveness is one of the best ways to show God's love to other people!

THOUGHT OF THE DAY

Don't try to do the math . . . the numbers can get pretty big. Just keep on forgiving!

PRAY TODAY

Dear God, help me to keep on forgiving others, just as You have forgiven me. Amen

WHAT a FRIEND!

"Just as the Father has loved Me, I have also loved you; abide in My love."

John 15:9 NASB

Do you know what friendship is about? Every true friendship should have kindness, thoughtfulness, love, and sharing. And there is no one who has given more of those things to you than Jesus.

That's right! Jesus is your friend. In fact, He's your very best friend of all.

Just like your other friends, Jesus wants to spend time with you. He wants to talk with you and listen to what you are excited about or the problems you are having. He cares about you more than anything. So don't forget to spend time with Him—there is no friend like Jesus!

THOUGHT OF THE DAY

Isn't it great that Jesus loves you so much?

PRAY TODAY

Dear God, I am glad that Jesus is my friend. Help me to remember to spend time with Him and be the best friend I can be. Amen.

Keep on Forgiving

"Rebuke your brother if he sins, and forgive him if he is sorry. Even if he wrongs you seven times a day and each time turns again and asks forgiveness, forgive him."

Luke 17:3-4 TLB

We all make mistakes and that's why we should be quick to forgive others. But sometimes, there are people in our lives that seem to need a lot of forgiveness!

Do you know someone who just keeps doing the same thing over and over, even if you've asked them to stop? Maybe they've hurt your feelings or called you names, but whatever they have done, Jesus said we should forgive them as many times as we need to.

After all, forgiveness helps you too! So just keep on forgiving, no matter what!

THOUGHT OF THE DAY

If your feelings get hurt by a friend, don't be afraid to talk to them about it. They might not realize how you feel!

PRAY TODAY

Dear God, please help me forgive as many times as I need to. Amen.

Help and Forgiveness

If we confess our sins, He is faithful and righteous to forgive us our sins and to cleanse us from all unrighteousness.

1 John 1:9 HCSB

D o you ever feel like you just keep making mistakes? If so, remember that nobody is perfect!

The important thing is to try your best to learn from your mistakes, so that you won't do the same things again. And the really good news is God always forgives you every single time you ask Him to. All you have to do is ask! So ask God for help and forgiveness, and don't worry about the rest.

THOUGHT OF THE DAY

Tomorrow is a brand new day!

PRAY TODAY

Dear God, please forgive me and help me make better choices next time. Amen.

GO TO GOD

The Lord says, "I will make you wise and show you where to go. I will guide you and watch over you."

Psalms 32:8 NCV

Sometimes being a kid is tough. There are always new things to learn and problems to solve. Sure, your parents help you anyway they can, but they can't be with you all the time.

So what should you do? There's only one solution–go to God! He is always with you and always knows what to do!

God promised to watch over you, guide you, and give you wisdom (the ability to know what is right and true) if you ask for it. So ask! God is waiting to help and show you just what you need to know.

THOUGHT OF THE DAY

If you want to know the answer, then don't be afraid to ask God the question!

PRAY TODAY

Dear God, help me remember that You are always ready to show me what to do and where to go. Amen.

Wait Patiently

And thus Abraham, having patiently waited, obtained the promise.

Hebrews 6:15 ESV

God made Abraham a promise. He promised Abraham that he would become a great nation and a great name, that God would bless everyone that blessed Abraham, and that because of Abraham, all the nations of the earth would be blessed.

That's a big promise! Especially since Abraham was already old and didn't have any children. But Abraham obeyed and trusted God and waited patiently.

Sure enough, everything God said came true. If you wait patiently, God's promises will happen for you, too!

THOUGHT OF THE DAY

God never forgets His promises—so don't give up!

PRAY TODAY

Dear God, thank You that you always keep your promises. Help me to wait patiently for You. Amen.

a new Song

Sing to the Lord a new song; sing to the Lord, all the earth. Sing to the Lord, praise his name; proclaim his salvation day after day.

Psalm 96:1-2 NIV

Have you praised God today? Praise is really singing, talking, and praying about how great God is and how much you love Him . . . and that is a great thing to do every day!

There are many ways to praise, but the Bible talks a lot about singing–and even singing a "new song." The good news is God doesn't worry about whether your voice sounds perfect or not, He just wants you to express the love you have in your heart. That is music to His ears! So make up a new song of your own today and let God know how much you love Him!

THOUGHT OF THE DAY

Praise is really just giving God much-deserved compliments!

PRAY TODAY

Dear God, thank You for everything You have done for me. You are a great and wonderful God! Amen.

THE PEACE OF GOD

Only God gives inward peace, and I depend on him.

Psalm 62:5 CEV

P eace is one of God's greatest gifts. God never wants you to worry or be afraid-of anything. Instead, He wants you to depend on Him.

When something starts to bother you, don't give in. Go to God and ask Him for help. Ask Him to fill you with His peace, and He will do it.

No matter what happens, the peace of God will get you through. You can always rely on Him!

THOUGHT OF THE DAY

God's peace lives on the inside of you. Nothing on the outside can take it away.

PRAY TODAY

Dear God, please fill me with Your peace today. Amen.

Confidence and Trust

Let your steadfast love, O Lord, be upon us, even as we hope in you.

Psalm 33:22 ESV

The Bible says that God has great plans for you. You are going to have an amazing future and do incredible things! But there will be days when you wonder if things are going right. Everybody has hard days . . . and that is when we need hope!

Hope means to have confidence and trust . . . and there is no one we can have more confidence or trust in than God. When you start to feel discouraged, choose to trust God. Remember how much He loves you and never give up.

THOUGHT OF THE DAY
What do you hope God will do for you in the future?

PRAY TODAY
Dear God, I will choose to trust You in everything. My hope is in You. Amen.

FOLLOW THE VOICE

My sheep hear My voice, I know them, and they follow Me.

John 10:27 HCSB

Shepherds have the job of protecting, feeding, and guiding the flock of sheep that are in their care. After a while, those sheep learn to recognize the voice of their shepherd and to trust him completely. They will follow that voice wherever it goes.

The Bible tells us that Jesus is our shepherd, and we are His sheep. Just like those other shepherds, Jesus is always protecting and caring for you, and as you get to know Jesus and learn to follow Him, you will begin to recognize His voice.

Listen closely . . . He is speaking to you!

THOUGHT OF THE DAY

The world is full of all kinds of voices–make sure you only follow your Shepherd!

PRAY TODAY

Dear God, thank You for Jesus, who is my Shepherd. Help me to always listen closely and follow where He leads me. Amen.

STAYING IN CONTROL

Don't let your spirit rush to be angry, for anger abides in the heart of fools.

Ecclesiastes 7:9 HCSB

Everybody gets angry sometimes. It's just a normal part of life. But when anger controls you instead of you controlling your anger, bad things can happen!

God wants us to learn how to handle our feelings and not be in such a big hurry to get angry. That means that when something happens that upsets you, make yourself slow down and think. Take some deep breaths and make sure you don't say anything that will make the situation worse.

If you make the effort to stay in control of yourself, even when you feel angry, everyone will be glad you did!

THOUGHT OF THE DAY

Kind words can change an awful lot of angry feelings.

PRAY TODAY

Dear God, please help me stay in control of my feelings, even when I am angry. Amen.

You Can Count on It

Do not be afraid or discouraged. For the LORD your God is with you wherever you go.

Joshua 1:9 NLT

God has made quite a few promises to us in the Bible, and He intends to keep every single one of them.

What are some of the promises He has made to you? He will give you rest. He will provide for all your needs. He will give you strength when you feel weak. He will never leave you. Nothing can separate you from His love. And most importantly, He has given you eternal life through Jesus!

God's promises never fail and they never grow old. They will always come true—you can count on it!

THOUGHT OF THE DAY
Wherever you go today, God is with you!

PRAY TODAY
Dear God, thank You for all of the promises You have made to me. Help me learn about them and always trust You. Amen.

WHO IS YOUR NEIGHBOR?

If you really fulfill the royal law according to the Scripture, "You shall love your neighbor as yourself," you are doing well.

James 2:8 ESV

The Bible tells us we should love our neighbor as ourselves, but who is God talking about?

Neighbors can be people who live on your street or in your neighborhood, but that's not all. Your neighbor is anyone that God brings across your path. They are the people you go to school with, the people in your church, the people in the checkout line at the store, and even those who live in other places!

Wherever you meet your neighbors, you can show your neighbors love in all kinds of ways. So who is your neighbor today?

THOUGHT OF THE DAY

How can you love a "neighbor" you've never even met? You can pray for them!

PRAY TODAY

Dear God, help me remember that anyone I meet is my "neighbor," so I can love them as I love myself. Amen.

Winning for God

"So you want first place? Then take the last place. Be the servant of all."

Mark 9:35 MSG

The world we live in cares a lot about winning and being the very best. But the kingdom of God works a little differently.

Jesus said that if we want to be "first," we have to be willing to be "last," and help others. And you can be the one to give it! But if we want to really know God and follow Him, we can't always think about ourselves.

There will always be someone who needs kindness, help, or encouragement. And you can be the one to give it! You might be the very person God needs to help change someone's life. Now that's winning!

THOUGHT OF THE DAY

God always sees when you put others first—and He loves it when you do!

PRAY TODAY

Dear God, I want to be like Jesus. Help me remember that "winning" isn't about me—it's about serving others. Amen.

Don't Hold Back

The righteous give without sparing.

Proverbs 21:26 NIV

The Bible talks a lot about giving to others. That's because it's important to God that we share and give freely so people will know how much He loves them.

To "give without sparing" means to give without holding anything back. Whether it's something that belongs to you or a simple act of kindness, God is pleased when you give everything you have to give.

The next time you have an opportunity to share, don't hold back! Then watch God do amazing things through you!

THOUGHT OF THE DAY

God never holds back when He gives good things to you!

PRAY TODAY

Dear God, please help me learn to give without holding anything back. Amen.

Say "Thank You"

Give thanks to the Lord, for He is good; His faithful love endures forever.

Psalm 106:1 HCSB

One of the first things we learn is how to say "please" and "thank you." But sometimes, we can forget to be thankful for the things we have.

It's important to remember to thank God for everything He has done for you . . . and your parents, too. After all, there are so many things to be thankful for! Your home, your family, your friends, your church, even your school! And most importantly, the great love that God has for you.

Give thanks to God today . . . He is good in every way!

THOUGHT OF THE DAY

Being thankful is a great way to remember how much you need God.

PRAY TODAY

Dear God, I am so thankful for everything You have given me. I love You. Amen.

ask for Help

If you don't know what you're doing, pray to the Father. He loves to help.

James 1:5 MSG

Do you ever find yourself in a pickle and don't know what to do? That's when it's time to pray!

There are lots of things that can make you unsure of the best thing to do: school and homework, relationships with family and friends, new places and activities. But God promised He would give us wisdom when we ask, and He really wants to help you. So whenever you have a problem–any kind of problem–take a moment and pray and ask God to help you. He loves to help!

THOUGHT OF THE DAY

Make a habit of praying first thing each morning and ask for God's help all day!

PRAY TODAY

Dear God, I am so glad that You have all the answers to my problems. I will ask You for help today. Amen.

Share and Give

Give generously, for your gifts will return to you later.

Ecclesiastes 11:1 NLT

Jesus told us that we should be generous with people, but there are times when we don't feel much like sharing. We want to keep the nice things we have all to ourselves. But God doesn't want selfishness to rule our hearts; He wants us to share and give generously.

God doesn't want us to love our "stuff" more than people. After all, that's not a very happy way to live!

Are you blessed to have nice things? If so, don't hold back–share your blessings with others. You might be surprised how happy it will make you feel!

THOUGHT OF THE DAY

Is your room cluttered with too many toys? Give some away!

PRAY TODAY

Dear God, I want to give and share whenever I can. Please help me be generous, kind, helpful, and grateful. Amen.

He Loves You That Much

For God so loved the world that he gave his only Son, so that everyone who believes in him will not perish but have eternal life.

John 3:16 NLT

Have you ever loved someone so much you were willing to do anything for them? God was willing to do everything for us! He held nothing back–even His son. That's how much God loves you!

So how big is God's love for you? It's not easy to describe or understand. But it's much bigger than anything you can imagine.

THOUGHT OF THE DAY

Can you think of three ways God shows His love for you every day?

PRAY TODAY

Dear God, I can't understand how much You love me, but I know You do. I love You, too! Amen.

The Best Way

I waited patiently for the Lord. He turned to me and heard my cry.

Psalm 40:1 NCV

God has very big things in store for you, and He knows the perfect moment for His plans to happen. Is God's "perfect moment" the same as yours? Maybe, but sometimes we have to be patient and wait.

For most people, being patient is really hard. We usually want what we want right now! But God's ways are different from ours and His way is always best. It's worth the wait for things to happen at just the right time.

So if God asks you to wait . . . then wait. And wait some more if you need to. You will be glad you did!

THOUGHT OF THE DAY

Doing things for others can make waiting a lot easier!

PRAY TODAY

Dear God, I know Your way is always the best. So if You ask me to wait, I will wait. Amen.

AnyThing is Possible

Jesus replied, "Why do you say 'if you can'? Anything is possible for someone who has faith!"

Mark 9:23 CEV

Whatever your dream may be–for now or in the future–anything is possible!

What others say about you, or even what you think about yourself, is not what you should count on. Instead, believe what God says about you! And God says in the Bible that anything is possible with Him. He's got great plans for you! And God never quits or gives up on you.

Put your faith in God, and believe that He wants what's best for you!

THOUGHT OF THE DAY

What's your dream? Do you talk to God about it?

PRAY TODAY

Dear God, You said anything is possible with faith. So I am going to keep my faith in You. Amen.

Nothing Like Family

His unchanging plan has always been to adopt us into his own family by sending Jesus Christ to die for us. And he did this because he wanted to!

Ephesians 1:5 TLB

There is nothing like family. In fact, having loving, kind, and healthy families was always God's plan.

God knew that no family would be perfect. And that's OK. The important thing is to keep loving each other and helping each other and having each other's back-no matter what.

What's even more exciting is that God wants all of us to be part of His own family, and that's why He sent Jesus. There's nothing better than that!

THOUGHT OF THE DAY

The Bible says God has adopted you into His family. Ask your parents about adoption and what it means.

PRAY TODAY

Dear God, I am so glad to be part of Your family. You are my Heavenly Father, and I love You. Amen.

WANT MORE PATIENCE?

God has chosen you and made you his holy people. He loves you. So always do these things: Show mercy to others, be kind, humble, gentle, and patient.

Colossians 3:12 NCV

Are you always perfectly patient with others? If so, great! But most of us have a hard time being patient sometimes. So if that's true for you, it's good to know that God is ready and willing to help you become a more patient person.

The Bible promises that when you ask for God's help, He will give you the things you need–and that includes patience! So, the next time you're in a big hurry or tired of waiting, ask God for help. He will give you the patience you need!

THOUGHT OF THE DAY

Having a hard time being patient? Think of all the times when others have to wait for you!

PRAY TODAY

Dear God, help me to slow down and be more patient with other people. Amen.

Happiness and Honesty

Lead a quiet and peaceable life in all godliness and honesty.

1 Timothy 2:2 KJV

Have you ever said something that wasn't true? When you did, were you sorry for what you said? Probably so.

When we're dishonest, we make ourselves unhappy in surprising ways. We can feel guilty, or the truth might come out, and we end up disappointing others and God. It's not hard to see that lies always cause more problems than they solve.

But happiness and honesty go hand in hand. If you choose to be truthful, you can choose to be happy!

THOUGHT OF THE DAY
What can you do to make it easier to be truthful?

PRAY TODAY
Dear God, let me always tell the truth, even when it's hard. Amen.

God's Love is Real

You are my God, and I will give you thanks; you are my God, and I will exalt you. Give thanks to the LORD, for he is good; his love endures forever.

Psalm 118:28-29 NIV

People often try to figure out if God is real. They look here and there, trying to find proof that He exists. But the best way to know that He exists is to know Him and receive His love in your heart.

God's love is real, and it's meant for you. In fact, God loves you so much that He sent His only Son to give His life for you so that you could be part of His family and live with Him and Jesus forever in heaven.

Once you've felt God's love, there can be no doubt that His love is real, and He is, too!

THOUGHT OF THE DAY

Nothing in the universe is greater than God's love!

PRAY TODAY

Dear God, thank You for loving me and for sending Your Son, Jesus, to die for me. Amen.

Nothing Like Joy

But let all those rejoice who put their trust in You; Let them ever shout for joy, because You defend them; Let those also who love Your name Be joyful in You.

Psalm 5:11 NKJV

There's nothing quite like the joy that God gives us! Joy is not a feeling based on what is happening to you or around you. Instead, it is the confident expectation of what God is going to do for you and how much He loves you.

What does that mean? That you know that God is going to come through for you; no matter what, He is going to work it out. God is bigger than everything.

Now, that's something to rejoice about!

THOUGHT OF THE DAY
The Bible says the joy of the Lord is your strength!

PRAY TODAY
Dear God, help me remember to look for joy in every situation. Amen.

TRUE LOVE

*There are three things that remain–faith, hope, and love–
and the greatest of these is love.*

1 Corinthians 13:13 TLB

What is true love? What God says about love is pretty different from what a lot of people think.

What God says tells us that true love is patient, kind, and loyal; never jealous, boastful, or proud. True love is not selfish or rude. It does not demand its own way. It is not irritable and does not hold grudges. True love hardly even notices when others do it wrong and is always happy when truth wins.

We can all use more of that kind of love!

THOUGHT OF THE DAY

Are there things you can work on to be better at love? What are they?

PRAY TODAY

Dear God, help me to love others the way You do. Amen.

KNOWING GOD

In the same way, we can see and understand only a little about God now, as if we were peering at his reflection in a poor mirror; but someday we are going to see him in his completeness, face-to-face.

1 Corinthians 13:12 TLB

Think for a minute . . . what do you know about God?

We know God created the whole universe, including the Earth and everything in it. We know God is love and sent Jesus to die for us, so we could be with Him forever. We know that He knows everything, sees everything, and makes anything possible.

The hard thing is that there is so much we don't know or understand. That's why faith is so important. Without faith, we couldn't know God at all! But the Bible says that some day, we are going to be able to see Him completely. That's going to be a great day!

THOUGHT OF THE DAY

One of the best ways to learn more about God is by reading and studying your Bible.

PRAY TODAY

Dear God, I want to know more about You. I just can't wait to see You for myself! Amen.

Put Him First

"So don't worry at all about having enough food and clothing. . . . But your heavenly Father already knows perfectly well that you need them, and he will give them to you if you give him first place in your life and live as he wants you to."

Matthew 6:31-33 TLB

How much stuff is too much stuff? Well, if you spend a lot of time worrying about the things you have, then you've got too much stuff! It's as simple as that.

God promised to take care of everything you will ever need, so there is no need to worry at all! He will always take care of you if you will put Him first!

So if you find yourself worrying too much about what you have or don't have, start thanking and praising God instead. Before you know it, all that stuff won't seem like such a big deal!

THOUGHT OF THE DAY

Think of three things you can thank God for today.

PRAY TODAY

Dear God, help me remember that what's really important is the love that I feel in my heart for my family and for You. Amen.

Be Patient and Kind

Always be humble and gentle. Be patient and accept each other with love.

Ephesians 4:2 ICB

Jesus said that we should treat other people in the same way that we want to be treated. And because we want other people to be patient and kind to us, we should be patient and kind to them, too.

Being patient with other people means treating them with kindness, respect, and understanding. It means waiting your turn when you're standing in line. It means forgiving your friends when they've done something you don't like. It means being kind even when you are tired or in a hurry. You can do that!

THOUGHT OF THE DAY

Patience and kindness always help others and you!

PRAY TODAY

Dear God, let me be patient with other people, just as You've been patient with me. Amen.

Finishing What You Start

We say they are happy because they did not give up.

James 5:11 NCV

Are you facing something that is really hard to do? Are you so frustrated that you just want to quit? Before you give up, remember that whatever your problem might be, God knows what to do and He will help you finish what you start!

Jesus set a good example for us to follow. He knew He was going to have to die on the cross—probably the hardest thing to do, ever—but He didn't give up. Instead, when He felt like He wanted to quit, Jesus asked God to help Him, and He kept going.

Don't worry, God will help you, too!

THOUGHT OF THE DAY

What's the hardest thing you've ever done? Aren't you glad you didn't give up?

PRAY TODAY

Dear God, sometimes it is really hard to keep going. Please help me finish and not give up. Amen.

WORDS OF KINDNESS

Lord, help me control my tongue; help me be careful about what I say.

Psalm 141:3 NCV

There's a saying that goes, "sticks and stones can break my bones, but words can never hurt me." The problem is that saying is wrong—words can hurt!

Everyone says things they don't mean sometimes, and when that happens, the best thing to do is ask for forgiveness and explain that you didn't mean what you said. But sometimes, it can be really hard to undo the hurt that our words can cause.

That's why God wants us to control our mouths and watch what we say. So do your best to use words of kindness, not words that hurt.

THOUGHT OF THE DAY

You are the only one who can choose your words—so choose wisely!

PRAY TODAY

Dear God, please help me remember that my words are important. I want to speak words that help! Amen.

Secrets for a Happy Life

Rejoice always! Pray constantly. Give thanks in everything, for this is God's will for you in Christ Jesus.

1 Thessalonians 5:16-18 HCSB

This Bible verse gives us three great things God wants us to do!

First, rejoice! Be glad for each day. Find something to be happy about today! Second, pray constantly. This doesn't have to be hard . . . just think of God as being right there with you, and never more than a thought away. Third, give thanks for everything. Everything. It's really as simple as that.

If you can do these three things every day, your life will never be the same!

THOUGHT OF THE DAY

Every time something special happens–big or small–write it down on a small piece of paper and put it in the jar. At the end of the year, you'll see how much God has done for you!

PRAY TODAY

Dear God, help me remember to thank You and talk with You every day. Amen.

DO GOOD DEEDS

A good person produces good deeds from a good heart.

Luke 6:45 NLT

It's always a good thing to do good deeds. You might think nobody notices when you do good things, but God does.

The story in the Bible about the Good Samaritan is a great example. A Samaritan man who was traveling saw an injured man by the side of the road. Nobody else had stopped to help him, but he helped him up, took him to the doctor, and paid for his bill until he was healed.

God loves it when we make choices like that. One good choice can make all the difference!

THOUGHT OF THE DAY

If you see someone who's hurt or in need, maybe it's time to perform a good deed!

PRAY TODAY

Dear God, when my family or friends need my help, please help me be kind and do what I can to help. Amen.

HOLD ON TO THE TRUTH

Let not mercy and truth forsake you; bind them around your neck, write them on the tablet of your heart.

Proverbs 3:3 NKJV

One of the things God really cares about is the truth. Jesus said He is the Way, the Truth, and the Life. The Bible also tells us that God cannot lie. He is the truth and always will be.

If you want to know God better and be close to Him, you have to hold on to the truth and turn away from any temptation to be dishonest or lie.

That's not always an easy thing to do, but it is so worth it. You will never regret choosing truth!

THOUGHT OF THE DAY

Why do you think lying can be so easy, while telling the truth can be so hard?

PRAY TODAY

Dear God, I know that being truthful is always the best choice. Please help me not give into the temptation to not tell the truth. Amen.

Jesus Loves You

Just as the Father has loved Me, I also have loved you. Remain in My love.

John 15:9 HCSB

The Bible makes this promise: Jesus loves you. No matter what happens in your life, even when things don't go the way they should—Jesus loves you.

Everything Jesus did when He came to Earth was because of His love for you. He left heaven behind; He lived here so He could love, heal, and help people; He died on the cross for you!

Everything Jesus does is because of His love for you. He wants you to welcome Him into your heart so you can be with Him forever. The decision is up to you!

THOUGHT OF THE DAY
God's love for you is perfect—He never messes up!

PRAY TODAY
Dear God, thank You for loving me always, no matter what. Amen.

FULL OF JOY

Shout with joy to the LORD, O earth! Worship the LORD with gladness. Come before him, singing with joy.

Psalm 100:1-2 NLT

Have you ever felt so joyful that you couldn't help singing a happy song to God? Hopefully so. After all, there are so many reasons to be joyful!

God has given you so many blessings–your family, friends, home, church, and pets are just the beginning. But even the hard things that He helps us with can be a reason to celebrate.

No matter what happens in your day, if you remember to be thankful, your heart will be full of joy. And that's a good reason to sing and shout!

THOUGHT OF THE DAY

Say "thank you" to God every day, even if it's just because He loves you!

PRAY TODAY

Dear God, thank You for giving me so many good things, and my life. I want to celebrate You today! Amen.

Make Time for God

I wait quietly before God, for my hope is in him.

Psalm 62:5 NLT

Every day, there are so many things you have to do! Maybe you have to get up, eat breakfast, get dressed, go to school, work hard, eat lunch, work some more, and come home. Or maybe you just have a lot of things to do at home!

If you take some time to spend with God, you'll realize it is the best part of your day. So, take a few minutes and have some quiet time with Him today!

THOUGHT OF THE DAY

Remember, whenever you want to talk with God, He's ready to listen!

PRAY TODAY

Dear God, I want to know more about You, so I am going to spend time with You today. Amen.

WHERE FAITH COMES FROM

So faith comes from hearing, that is, hearing the Good News about Christ.

Romans 10:17 NLT

Have you ever wondered where faith comes from? It's pretty simple, really. Faith comes from hearing the good news about Jesus.

Once you hear the Word of God, it goes down into your heart like a seed. And before you know it, faith begins to spring up. Then, the more you hear, the stronger your faith grows.

There are so many ways you can hear the Word–at church, spending time with God, reading the Bible. If you will do these things, you'll have more faith than you know what to do with!

THOUGHT OF THE DAY

What is your favorite scripture about Jesus?

PRAY TODAY

Dear God, thank You for giving me ears to hear about Jesus and Your love for me. Amen.

Nothing Left to Fear

There is no fear in love, but perfect love casts out fear.

1 John 4:18 ESV

Being fearful is not fun. It can make you anxious and timid, and keep you from trying new things or trusting God. That's why God does not want you to be afraid!

God is love. And the Bible tells us that the perfect love of God casts out fear. That means that fear has to go when God's love is in you!

The secret to overcoming fear is trusting God. Trust Him completely. Believe with all your heart that He loves you and protects you and cares for you all the time. If you really believe that, there is nothing left to fear!

THOUGHT OF THE DAY
Faith and trust are the opposite of fear.

PRAY TODAY
Dear God, thank You for Your perfect love that takes away all fear. Amen.

When You Don't Know What To Say

Say only what helps, each word a gift.

Ephesians 4:29 MSG

Our words can be a gift to someone! They can give someone a happy moment. God can use you to help if you speak words that help and heal.

What can you say? Something like, "Smile, I feel bad when you're sad," "I like it when we play together," "I like to talk to you," or "I'm praying for you." Even better, "God loves you very much."

Whatever you say, choose words that bring comfort and love, and they will be a wonderful gift.

THOUGHT OF THE DAY

One way to find the right words is to pray and ask God what to say.

PRAY TODAY

Dear God, please help me to find the right words at the right time. Amen.

BROTHERLY LOVE

Love one another with brotherly affection. Outdo one another in showing honor.

Romans 12:10 ESV

Friendship is one of the very best gifts that God has given us.

The Bible tells us to love each other with "brotherly love." Do you have a brother, or maybe a sister? If not, you should know that no one loves you quite as much as a brother or a sister. They love you no matter what.

Friends that love you like that are the kind of friends you want to have, and the kind of friend you want to be!

THOUGHT OF THE DAY

Love your friends like they are an important part of your family!

PRAY TODAY

Dear God, thank You for my friends. Help me to be the kind of friend I would want to have. Amen.

JUST RELAX

"I know that you can do all things, and that no purpose of yours can be thwarted."

Job 42:2 ESV

There may be days when you think everything just seems to be going wrong, but that's when you need to remember that God has a plan!

God has a perfect plan for everyone and everything–and God's plans always come to pass. Why? Because He is God, of course!

Our plans may fail, but God's never do. So, when you can't understand how things are ever going to work out, just relax and trust God. Then watch and see what happens!

THOUGHT OF THE DAY

God's got it all under control!

PRAY TODAY

Dear God, I'm glad You have a plan and that Your plans always happen just the way You want them to. Amen.

GOD IS GOOD

Surely goodness and mercy shall follow me all the days of my life, and I shall dwell in the house of the Lord forever.

Psalm 23:6 ESV

One thing that is always true about God: He is good! The Bible says that every good thing comes down from our Father in heaven.

If you look for the good, you can't help but find things–big and small–that are gifts from God to you. God is good, all the time!

THOUGHT OF THE DAY

Ask God to help you see His goodness in every day.

PRAY TODAY

Dear God, thank You for Your goodness to me and my family. I love You. Amen.

WORKING HARD

Work hard and cheerfully at all you do, just as though you were working for the Lord and not merely for your masters.

Colossians 3:23 TLB

Have your parents ever asked you to work hard and do your very best? If so, that was good advice! Learn to work hard at whatever you do and you will succeed for the rest of your life.

One thing that can help is to remember that everything you do is for God. Even if you don't think anyone else notices your efforts, He always does and wants to bless you. So keep up the hard work!

THOUGHT OF THE DAY

Hard work always reaps a good reward!

PRAY TODAY

Dear God, please help me remember to work hard, even if I don't like something. I want to make You happy even if I don't want to do it. Amen.

Keep Your Heart Pure

Blessed are the pure in heart, for they shall see God.

Matthew 5:8 ESV

God cares an awful lot about the condition of our hearts. Why? Because our hearts are the core of who we really are.

Your heart is what makes you unique and special. It is also where your thoughts, feelings, and words come from. Everything we do and say begins in our hearts. That's why God wants us to make sure we keep our hearts full of His love.

You can keep your heart pure by forgiving others, asking God for forgiveness, and thinking about good things—especially what God says.

THOUGHT OF THE DAY

When it comes to your heart, what goes in is what comes out!

PRAY TODAY

Dear God, please help me keep my heart full of good things. Amen.

Heaven is FOR Real

But, as it is written, "What no eye has seen, nor ear heard, nor the heart of man imagined, what God has prepared for those who love him."

1 Corinthians 2:9 ESV

What do you think Heaven is like? There are things we know about Heaven, because the Bible gives us some hints: the streets are made out of gold; there is no pain or suffering or sickness; God has built many mansions for us to live in; and it is a place full of joy!

The Bible also tells us that God has done things for us that we cannot even imagine. What does that mean? That no matter what wonderful things you can think of, Heaven is even better!

But no matter what awaits us, one thing is certain: Heaven is for real!

THOUGHT OF THE DAY

Heaven is a wonderful place!

PRAY TODAY

Dear God, thank You for making Heaven so I could live with You. I know it is going to be wonderful! Amen.

Laugh out Loud

He will yet fill your mouth with laughter, and your lips with shouting.

Job 8:21 ESV

There is nothing that makes your day better than a good laugh. Especially the kind that you just can't seem to stop and makes your belly hurt!

God loves it when you have fun and laugh out loud. He made you to be joyful and experience all kinds of wonderful things.

If you tend to take things a little too seriously sometimes, lighten up! Do something spontaneous just for fun or hang out with your best friends. Just make sure you make time for lots of laughter!

THOUGHT OF THE DAY

Laughter is like medicine: it makes you feel better!

PRAY TODAY

Dear God, I love to laugh. Please help me remember that laughter is the best medicine. Amen.

PeRFeCT Peace

You keep him in perfect peace whose mind is stayed on you, because he trusts in you.

Isaiah 26:3 ESV

Did you know that God has peace that is perfect? It can be hard to understand what that is like.

The good news is that God's perfect peace can be yours—all day every day. And God tells us how to receive it: trust Him completely and keep your thoughts on Him.

With God, you never have to worry or be afraid. His peace is the perfect answer for every situation!

THOUGHT OF THE DAY

Always trust God—He will never let you down!

PRAY TODAY

Dear God, thank You for Your perfect peace. I will trust You and think about all You have done for me.
Amen.

The Light Always Wins

The light shines in the darkness, and the darkness has not overcome it.

John 1:5 ESV

Alight brightens up darkness. Jesus is a bright light in our world! Even a tiny match can light up a dark room and Jesus is so much brighter and stronger than a match!

The Bible says that darkness cannot "overcome" the Light, which means darkness cannot defeat the Light.

If we remember to look for Jesus, and help others see Him too, we will never be overcome by darkness. The light of Jesus always wins!

THOUGHT OF THE DAY

If you love Jesus, you have His light inside you, too!

PRAY TODAY

Dear God, help me to always look for Your light in every dark situation. Amen.

Small Choices

"Thus says the Lord of hosts, Render true judgments, show kindness and mercy to one another."

Zechariah 7:9 ESV

One of the most important things you can do every day is show kindness and mercy to others.

How do you do that? By saying nice words and doing kind things for the people you meet. Showing mercy means that you are quick to forgive and help people when they are in trouble.

The small choices we make every day, like choosing to share or telling someone how much God loves them, can have big results. They are the very things God can use to change someone's life!

THOUGHT OF THE DAY

Has someone shown you kindness lately? How can you do the same for someone else?

PRAY TODAY

Dear God, please show me how to make kind and merciful choices every day. Amen.

DO THE RIGHT THING

Those who want to do right more than anything else are happy. God will fully satisfy them.

Matthew 5:6 ICB

If you're like most people, you probably have been tempted to do things you know you shouldn't, especially if your friends are all doing it. But just because your friends make a choice that doesn't seem right, doesn't mean that you have to do the same thing.

Your parents and teachers have worked hard to teach you what is right and what isn't, and God really wants you to listen and do your best to do what they say.

So don't go along with a bad choice. Instead, do the right thing. You'll be glad you did . . . and so will God!

THOUGHT OF THE DAY

Never give in to pressure that feels wrong. Just say, "no, thank you."

PRAY TODAY

Dear God, please help me make right choices and not give in to temptation. Amen.

GOD'S LOVE IS PERFECT

No one has ever seen God; if we love one another, God abides in us and his love is perfected in us.

1 John 4:12 ESV

God does not want you worrying about everything you do having to "be perfect." The Bible tells us that no one has ever been perfect–except Jesus. That is why we all need Him!

If you are trying to be perfect in everything you say and do, you will only get frustrated and discouraged. It's simply not possible!

The good news is that God is helping you, and if you do your best to follow Him, He will make His love perfect in you. You just have to trust Him and He will do the rest!

THOUGHT OF THE DAY

God loves you just the way you are!

PRAY TODAY

Dear God, help me not worry about being "perfect." Instead I will do my best and trust You. Amen.

Guard Your Heart

For out of the overflow of the heart the mouth speaks.

Matthew 12:34 NIV

Have you ever said something in a hurry without thinking about what you were going to say? Sometimes words come out that we don't intend to say or aren't the best words to use.

The Bible says that our words come from our heart—and that is especially true when we are under pressure. If you are scared or mad or excited, sometimes it's hard to stop and think about what you are going to say, and whatever's going on in your heart will come out.

So guard your heart and pray, and ask God to give you good thoughts and words.

THOUGHT OF THE DAY

If you put God's words from the Bible in your heart, that is what will come out.

PRAY TODAY

Dear God, please help me watch what I say, and most importantly, give me a good, clean heart. Amen.

a Praise Break

Praise the LORD. Give thanks to the LORD, for he is good; his love endures forever.

Psalm 106:1 NIV

If you're like most kids, you're probably really busy going, learning, and doing things. But no matter how busy you are—even if you hardly have a moment to spare—you should still slow down long enough to say "Thank You," to God every day.

God has given you so many wonderful things, and it makes Him glad when we remember His goodness to us with thankful hearts. What can you think of right now that God has done for you? Now, go ahead . . . take a praise break!

THOUGHT OF THE DAY

There's never a bad time to praise God!

PRAY TODAY

Dear God, thank You for everything You have done for me. Amen.

Where Your Treasure is

"The place where your treasure is, is the place you will most want to be, and end up being."

Matthew 6:21 MSG

What is your "treasure"? In other words, what are the most precious, important things to you?

The Bible says we shouldn't make our treasure all kinds of material things, like toys or clothes or gadgets. We can't take any of it with us to Heaven, anyway. Instead, we should focus on the things that are important to God. Things like family, friends, and telling people about Jesus.

Those are the best treasures of all, because that's what will last forever!

THOUGHT OF THE DAY
What are your "forever" treasures?

PRAY TODAY
Dear God, help me remember what's really important, and what's not. Amen.

Staying Safe

Losing self-control leaves you as helpless as a city without a wall.

Proverbs 25:28 CEV

The Bible talks a lot about self-control. It is one of the things that we begin to develop when we know God, like kindness, respect, joy, and peace.

When we lose control of ourselves–whether our words, feelings, or actions–really bad things can happen, to you and to others. You might hurt someone's feelings, or worse, someone or something could get hurt.

God wants you to be safe, and using self-control protects you from all kind of trouble. Just remember, self-control takes lots of practice, so keep working at it!

THOUGHT OF THE DAY

One way to practice self-control is to wait when you really want something. Just put it on hold for a bit!

PRAY TODAY

Dear God, thank You for helping me get better at self-control so I can be safe and happy. Amen.

Run for the Finish Line

Let us run with endurance the race that is set before us.

Hebrews 12:1 ESV

Have you ever run a race? Or maybe watched someone else running or racing on TV? Would it make sense if they stopped just a bit from the finish line and quit? Of course not!

Life is a lot like a race. Sometimes we have shorter things to do and sometimes our goals or jobs take a long time, but if you quit, give up, or even worse, forget about the finish line that is up ahead, you miss out on all the fun!

And just because you are a kid doesn't mean you don't have important things to accomplish. Just keep going and run for the finish line!

THOUGHT OF THE DAY

If you are tempted to give up, focus on small steps that you can accomplish one at a time.

PRAY TODAY

Dear God, help me remember that there is a finish line ahead when I get tired or discouraged. Amen.

Good Habits

I can do anything I want to if Christ has not said no, but some of these things aren't good for me.

1 Corinthians 6:12 TLB

There are all kinds of habits–good ones and bad ones. Good habits can help us have a happy, healthy life, but bad habits can often lead to problems and take away from you becoming everything God wants you to be.

Everyone can benefit from good habits, like eating healthy food, exercising every day, getting plenty of sleep, spending time with your family, and going to church. There are probably a few not-so-good habits you could change, too. Ask your parents for help and look for ways to make better choices. You'll be happy you did!

THOUGHT OF THE DAY

Starting a good new habit takes a lot of work, but in a couple of weeks it won't seem so hard!

PRAY TODAY

Dear God, please help me make new, good habits so I can be everything You want me to be. Amen.

Run from Temptation

Run from temptations that capture young people. Always do the right thing.

2 Timothy 2:22 CEV

Joseph was an important man in the Bible, and the story of his life is pretty amazing. One time he literally ran away from temptation.

Joseph worked for an important man named Potiphar, and Potiphar's wife wanted Joseph to do things that were wrong. Joseph said no, but she kept trying to tempt him anyway. So what did he do? He ran away! In fact, he ran so fast that he left his coat dangling in her hands!

Sometimes, running away is the only way to beat temptation!

THOUGHT OF THE DAY

When you are tempted to do something wrong, you need to be ready to run!

PRAY TODAY

Dear God, I want to please You and not give into temptation. Help me know when it's just best to run away. Amen.

Complete Trust

Trust in the Lord with all your heart; do not depend on your own understanding.

Proverbs 3:5 NLT

Do you remember the story of how the angel Gabriel told Mary that she was going to have a baby? And not just any baby, but the son of God?

Mary couldn't understand how she could have a baby when she wasn't married, but when the angel told her that God was going to do it through the Holy Spirit, she trusted him completely. That took great faith!

Because of Mary's great faith and trust, God was able to use her to bring about the greatest miracle ever and she became the mother of Jesus. He wants to use you too!

THOUGHT OF THE DAY

God can do anything He wants to do, so don't doubt Him!

PRAY TODAY

Dear God, help me remember Mary when I feel like something is impossible, and trust You. Amen.

ask for Wisdom

Ask for wisdom, it shall be given unto you . . .

Proverbs 10:23 NCV

D o you want to be wise? Would you like to be able to make really good decisions and figure out how to solve all kinds of problems? Then ask God!

The Bible says if we want wisdom, we just need to ask God for it. What a smart idea!

Everyone has times when they don't know what to do. Whether you have a problem with another person or something you need to do that you can't figure out, take a moment and ask God to give you wisdom. It just might make everything easier!

THOUGHT OF THE DAY

Read the book of Proverbs in the Bible. It is full of godly wisdom!

PRAY TODAY

Dear God, I wish I understood everything, but I don't. Please give me Your wisdom. Amen.

Keeping Faith Alive

In the same way, faith by itself, if it is not accompanied by action, is dead.

James 2:17 NIV

If you believe in God and His Son, Jesus, then you have faith. When you first begin to learn about God, your faith might be small, but it is very real.

Then, as your faith grows, it becomes important to start acting on what you believe if you want to keep your faith growing.

You probably already know how to do that: by showing kindness to others, by giving and sharing freely, by caring for people. When others see God's love through you by how you treat them, they will know your faith is alive and well!

THOUGHT OF THE DAY

Do you have a neighbor that you can help or do something nice for?

PRAY TODAY

Dear God, please help me put actions to my faith. Amen.

Don't Worry, Be Happy!

Worry weighs a person down; an encouraging word cheers a person up.

Proverbs 12:25 NLT

Do you ever have trouble sleeping because you're worried about something? Maybe you have to do a hard assignment at school. Or maybe someone you know isn't being very nice. Whatever might be troubling you, you don't have to let it bother you!

God wants you to give Him your worries, so He can take care of the problems. Then you can be happy and enjoy your day, or your sleep!

All you have to do is pray and give it to God. You will feel so much better!

THOUGHT OF THE DAY

Focus on God and worry will seem far away.

PRAY TODAY

Dear God, please take my worries and problems from me. I'll let You take care of them. Amen.

THE RIGHT WORDS

Be gracious in your speech. The goal is to bring out the best in others in a conversation, not put them down, not cut them out.

Colossians 4:6 MSG

The words you speak make a difference! They can either help or hurt, tear down or build up, encourage or bring someone down.

God wants us to use our words in the best way possible. That means, when we speak, we should always choose to say things that make others feel better.

Bringing out the best in people is not hard–just remember to use kind, thoughtful words. And if you always speak to people the way you want to be spoken to, you won't have any trouble finding the right words.

THOUGHT OF THE DAY

Always think before you speak!

PRAY TODAY

Dear God, I want to always speak words that please You. Please help me choose them carefully. Amen.

encourage every Day

You must encourage one another each day.

Hebrews 3:13 CEV

Everyone needs encouragement sometimes! None of us can do everything, and we all have some kind of struggle that we deal with—that's just how life is.

How do you feel when someone tells you, "You are going to make it!" "You can do it—just keep going!" "You are awesome and God is on your side!" Sounds pretty great, doesn't it?

Even if you are having a great day, chances are that someone around you is having a hard time. So keep an eye out for someone that might need some encouragement, and then let them have it!

THOUGHT OF THE DAY

Encouraging others is really about giving them some of your confidence.

PRAY TODAY

Dear God, please give me the right words of encouragement that people need to hear. Amen.

Lions and Bears

Sir, I have killed lions and bears that way, and I can kill this worthless Philistine. He shouldn't have made fun of the army of the living God!

1 Samuel 17:36 CEV

David was brave. If you've heard the story about David and Goliath, then that probably doesn't surprise you. But David learned how to be brave when he was still a kid, just doing his job–watching the sheep.

Doesn't sound very exciting, does it? David probably would have preferred to be doing something else, but he had to protect the flock.

God was preparing David for what He was supposed to do. David even had to kill a lion and a bear with his bare hands! He learned to be brave caring for the sheep, and it helped make him a hero and a great king.

THOUGHT OF THE DAY
The things you do now can change your future!

PRAY TODAY
Dear God, I don't know what You have planned for me, but You do. Help me be ready. Amen.

everything you need

And my God will supply every need of yours according to his riches in glory in Christ Jesus.

Philippians 4:19 ESV

Can you think of anything that God doesn't have? Of course not! The Bible says the Earth is the Lord's; that He even owns all the cattle on every hill.

The problem is sometimes we forget that everything belongs to God, and we start to worry about how we are going to get what we need.

But the Bible says that God will take care of everything. That's a pretty big thing to say! But God is a very big God. And He has more than enough to give you everything you need!

THOUGHT OF THE DAY

Don't worry . . . your Heavenly Father has got you covered!

PRAY TODAY

Dear God, thank You for taking care of all my needs. I will trust You and not worry. Amen.

GOD KNOWS

Work hard and with gladness all the time, as though working for Christ, doing the will of God with all your hearts.

Ephesians 6:7 TLB

God wants you to think of Him when you are doing the things you have to do, and work hard at them with a good attitude. God knows and sees everything, and He also knows how you feel about it.

So if you work hard as though you are doing it all for God, your efforts will never go unrewarded–and that hard work won't seem quite so hard!

THOUGHT OF THE DAY

Every time you do your best, you make your Father God proud!

PRAY TODAY

Dear God, I want to make You proud of me by working hard with a happy attitude. Amen.

WHAT a BLESSING

"But blessed are those who trust in the Lord and have made the Lord their hope and confidence."

Jeremiah 17:7 NLT

If you know God, then you are truly blessed!

What does it mean to be blessed? To be truly happy and at peace in your heart, no matter what is happening around you. To know how important you are to God and to be loved by Him no matter what. To know that God has a plan for your life, and everything that matters to you matters to Him. To have everything you need given to you and even the secret hopes of your heart come to pass.

What a blessing it is to be blessed by God!

THOUGHT OF THE DAY

The greatest blessing is to share God's love with others.

PRAY TODAY

Dear God, thank You for blessing me. I am so thankful for who You are and everything You have done. Amen.

LOVING GOD

This is love for God: to obey his commands.

1 John 5:3 NIV

Have you ever wondered why it's so important to obey your parents? Aside from the fact that they really care about you and want to keep you happy and safe, obeying your parents also shows them how much you love and respect them.

The same is true for God. He also really cares about you and wants you to be happy and safe. And He knows even more than your parents do about the dangers and problems that could lie ahead. Obeying God is one of the very best ways you can show how much you love Him.

THOUGHT OF THE DAY

If you trust God, obeying Him is a great way to show it!

PRAY TODAY

Dear God, I want to obey You and honor You, so You will know how much I love You. Amen.

Make Things Right with God

People who conceal their sins will not prosper, but if they confess and turn from them, they will receive mercy.

Proverbs 28:13 NLT

King David was a mighty hero of Israel and a man who truly loved God. But he made some mistakes in his life.

It's true that everyone makes mistakes, but David made some big ones. And you might think that God wouldn't be able to use him after that. But David did three important things right: he didn't make any excuses, he was truly sorry and sincerely asked God to forgive him, and he loved God more than anything else.

David knew he had messed up and he was determined to make things right with God. And that made all the difference!

THOUGHT OF THE DAY

Nothing is impossible for God, not even when we mess up!

PRAY TODAY

Dear God, I am so glad that You forgive me for all my mistakes and always give me another chance. Amen.

Love and Loyalty

But Ruth said, "Do not urge me to leave you or to return from following you. For where you go I will go, and where you lodge I will lodge. Your people shall be my people, and your God my God."

Ruth 1:16 ESV

What comes to mind when you think of your family? Love? Laughter? Holidays and spending fun times together?

All of these things are true and part of the reason why God made families. Another important one is loyalty.

Loyalty is when you stick by someone no matter what. Ruth in the Bible showed what true loyalty is supposed to be. She refused to leave her mother-in-law, even though they went through some really hard times. But because of Ruth's loyalty, God did amazing things and took care of her and her family. If you give your loyalty to God and your family, He will do the same for you!

THOUGHT OF THE DAY

Loyalty is always standing by someone, no matter what.

PRAY TODAY

Dear God, thank You for my family. Help me to always be loyal and true to them and You. Amen.

Where You Can Hide

You are my hiding place and my shield; I hope in your word.

Psalm 119:114 NCV

God is your hiding place. That means that no matter where you are–He is the safe place you can run to. The Bible also calls God a rock we can stand on, and a shelter from the storm. You might need to use your imagination a bit to understand what these examples mean for you, but there's no safer place to be than with God.

THOUGHT OF THE DAY

When you hide yourself in God, nothing bothers you like it did before.

PRAY TODAY

Dear God, Help me remember to look for You whenever I need help. Amen.

a Special Friend

I praise you, for I am fearfully and wonderfully made. Wonderful are your works; my soul knows it very well.

Psalm 139:14 ESV

Do you know someone who is a bit different from you? Maybe they look different, or act different, or were born with a problem that some kids don't have? Growing up can be hard for everybody, but it can be really hard for kids who have special needs.

You may not understand why some kids look or act the way they do, but you can be sure what they need most is a good friend. Make an effort to get to know them and learn about what they like and what makes them unique and special. If you do, you'll find that you have found a special friend indeed.

THOUGHT OF THE DAY

If you aren't sure why someone seems different, ask your parents privately to help you understand.

PRAY TODAY

Dear God, I know You love everyone the same. Help me share Your love with everyone—even if they are different from me. Amen.

Stand Up for What You Believe in

"Be strong! Be courageous! Do not be afraid of them! For the Lord your God will be with you. He will neither fail you nor forsake you."

Deuteronomy 31:6 TLB

The Bible tells the story of Daniel, who loved and served God, even though almost everyone around him did not. Then, one day he stood up for what he knew was right–that only the one true God should be worshipped.

People were not happy. Daniel was thrown into the lion's den as punishment, and everyone was certain he would be killed. After all, no one had ever survived a pack of hungry lions before. But God shut the lions' mouths, and Daniel was saved.

Standing up for what you believe in can take a lot of courage, but God will stand with you.

THOUGHT OF THE DAY

Courage is doing the right thing even when you are afraid.

PRAY TODAY

Dear God, I hope I never have to face lions, but please help me to have the courage to stand up for You. Amen.

How to Pray

Do not be like them, for your Father knows what you need before you ask him. Pray then like this: "Our Father in heaven, hallowed be your name. Your kingdom come, your will be done, on earth as it is in heaven."

Matthew 6:8-10 ESV

Are there times when you don't know how to pray or what to say? Everyone feels like that sometimes. Even Jesus' disciples weren't sure how they were supposed to pray, so Jesus had to teach them.

If you read the Lord's Prayer in the Bible, it will help you. First, praise God and thank Him for who He is. Then, pray that His will would be done in the Earth. Next, ask God for the things that you need, and for forgiveness for your sin. Finally, ask God to help you avoid temptation.

Those things are important, and so is telling God whatever is in your heart.

THOUGHT OF THE DAY

Praying is as much about listening to God as it is about talking to Him.

PRAY TODAY

Dear God, thank You for always listening to me when I pray. Help me hear what You have to say to me, too. Amen.

WHAT YOU CAN DO

Jesus looked at them and said, "With man this is impossible, but with God all things are possible."

Matthew 19:26 NIV

Are there some things you wish you could do better? Probably so. The good news is that God doesn't look at what you can't do, He sees what you can do with Him!

That's what happened to Moses in the Bible. Moses made a lot of mistakes and he wasn't good at talking to people, but God had a plan for him! God used the things Moses could do to lead his people out of Egypt and into the Promised Land.

THOUGHT OF THE DAY

With God, all things are possible!

PRAY TODAY

Dear God, help me not to doubt what You can do in my life. Amen.

a Special Promise

"Honor your father and mother. Then you will live a long, full life in the land the Lord your God is giving you."

Exodus 20:12 NLT

The Ten Commandments have a lot of wisdom for how to live your life and you should do your best to follow all of them. But there is one that is a little different, and that is the fifth commandment, which says "Honor your father and mother."

What makes this commandment special is that it is the only one that contains a promise. The Bible says if you honor your parents, you will have a long and full life.

The next time you are tempted to talk back or be disrespectful to your parents, stop and think. Respecting them is always the best way to go!

THOUGHT OF THE DAY

Every choice has a consequence. Pick the right one!

PRAY TODAY

Dear God, please help me be respectful and kind to my parents. Amen.

THE FRUIT OF THE SPIRIT

But the fruit of the Spirit is love, joy, peace, patience, kindness, goodness, faithfulness, gentleness, self-control; against such things there is no law.

Galatians 5:22-23 ESV

When you decide to follow Jesus, the Holy Spirit comes to live inside you. When that happens, some things start to change.

Before you know it, you don't get mad so much, and instead you begin to feel peace and love for others in a new way. You begin to use more self-control and become more gentle with people. And you look for ways to be kind to people–even those that aren't so nice to you.

The Holy Spirit is making fruit in you!

THOUGHT OF THE DAY

What's growing on the inside of you?

PRAY TODAY

Dear God, thank You for changing me on the inside and helping me grow the fruit of the Spirit. Amen.

GiFTS FROM GOD

As each has received a gift, use it to serve one another, as good stewards of God's varied grace.

1 Peter 4:10 ESV

God makes everyone with their own set of special gifts and abilities. Do you have some idea of what yours are? Perhaps you like to dance, sing, draw, build, or play a sport. Maybe you love animals or working with plants.

Whatever it is that you love to do, thank God for giving you those gifts—and then practice, practice, practice!

If you will be willing to work hard to develop your unique gifts, God will be able to use you in amazing ways. And that is worth all the time and effort!

THOUGHT OF THE DAY

A talent should never be wasted. Find a way to use it!

PRAY TODAY

Dear God, thank You for the gifts You have given me. Please help me work hard and not waste them. Amen.

CONFIDENCE FROM GOD

For the Lord will be your confidence, and will keep your foot from being caught.

Proverbs 3:26 NKJV

Confidence is trusting that you can do something and the result will be good. God wants us to know we can have confidence in Him—He always loves us and He is true to His word.

If you believe you can do it, God will be right there helping you. Be confident God can help and you can do big things.

THOUGHT OF THE DAY

God's Word is our source of confidence.

PRAY TODAY

Dear God, I know You have given me many gifts, but please help me remember to always put my confidence in You. Amen.

DOING GREAT THINGS TOGETHER

Two are better than one, because they have a good reward for their toil.

Ecclesiastes 4:9 ESV

None of us are meant to do things on our own--we all need each other, every day. Can you imagine how hard your life would be if you had to do everything by yourself? That wouldn't be very fun at all!

The Bible says "two are better than one," and it's true. Working with someone else can make a huge difference in how things go and end up. There is nothing quite like teamwork.

God loves teamwork . . . because we can do great things together!

THOUGHT OF THE DAY

What are some ways you can help others?

PRAY TODAY

Dear God, help me find ways to be kind and helpful to others. I want them to know how much You love them. Amen.

The Power of Praise

I will bless the Lord at all times; his praise shall continually be in my mouth.

Psalm 34:1 ESV

What is it like to praise God? Joy. Thankfulness. Happiness. Blessing. All of these things are rolled up into every moment that we praise God by telling Him how great He is and how much we love Him.

Nothing makes your relationship with God quite as wonderful as praise. When you praise God, He hears you and answers you. He pours out all the blessings of heaven upon you. And before you know it, whatever troubles or problems you may be dealing with don't seem so bad. There is really nothing as powerful as praise!

THOUGHT OF THE DAY

Praise God all the time, everywhere, and every day!

PRAY TODAY

Dear God, You are a great God and I love You. Thank You for taking care of me. Amen.

CHANGING THE WORLD

For the whole law is fulfilled in one word: "You shall love your neighbor as yourself."

Galatians 5:14 ESV

One of the best ways to make your life better–and the people around you, too–is by practicing the Golden Rule. Jesus told us to always do for others what we would want them to do for us. Don't you think if everyone did that, the world be a much better place?

Sadly, too many people don't honor the Golden Rule. But if you choose to practice it in your own life, before you know it the love of God will start to spread from you to person after person, until you have changed so many lives, one at a time. That's a world-changer!

THOUGHT OF THE DAY

Is there a way you can be kinder to your friends?

PRAY TODAY

Dear God, help me to always remember the truth of the Golden Rule and follow it. Amen.

a Happy Life

*Be content with what you have, because God has said,
"Never will I leave you; never will I forsake you."*

Hebrews 13:5 NIV

Where can you find happiness? Does it come from being famous or having lots of stuff? Nope. Does it come from always getting your way? Definitely not. Real happiness is a gift from God to those who trust Him, spend time with Him, and do their best to do what He says.

If we can't find happiness in God, we will never find it anywhere else. But, if you look for Him and obey Him, you will have a joyful, peaceful, and meaningful life. God loves to give His children good things-especially joy, peace, and a happy heart!

THOUGHT OF THE DAY

Trust God and do your best-and He will take care of the rest!

PRAY TODAY

Dear God, I know You want me to be happy. Help me to trust You and follow You now and forever. Amen.

HeaLTHy HabiTS

Don't you know that you are God's temple and that God's Spirit lives in you?

1 Corinthians 3:16 NCV

The Bible has clear instructions about taking care of yourself. You see, God gave you a wonderful, amazing, one-of-a-kind body, and He wants you to take good care of it. So it's important to start learning to make good choices.

Can you think of ten things you can do to take care of your body? Here are some ideas to get you started: 1. Eat healthy food. 2. Always buckle your seatbelt. 3. Get plenty of sleep. What others can you think of?

Your body is a precious gift, so start making some smart and healthy habits!

THOUGHT OF THE DAY

Make one small, healthy change in your habits this week.

PRAY TODAY

Dear God, thank You for giving me this body to live in. Help me to do everything I can to keep it strong and healthy. Amen.

Be Thankful for Friends

I give thanks to my God for every remembrance of you.

Philippians 1:3 HCSB

What are some of your favorite things you love about your friends? What do you like to do together? Are there hobbies or common interests that you share? How do they make you feel when you spend time together?

Just like the Bible says, we should thank God every time we remember the special friends He has given us. Each one is important and can never be replaced.

Today, give thanks to God for all the people who love you, both family and friends.

THOUGHT OF THE DAY

Write a note to a friend and tell them how important they are to you.

PRAY TODAY

Dear God, thank You for my special friends. Help me to always be a good friend to others, too. Amen.

Keep Smiling!

Happiness makes a person smile, but sadness can break a person's spirit.

Proverbs 15:13 NCV

Everybody likes to see a happy, smiling face . . . and you will feel better when you smile, too! So the next time you find yourself thinking about things that make you frown, ask God to help you be thankful.

Don't forget to count your blessings. How many wonderful things do you have to be thankful for? And, while you're at it, remember that God has promised to love you always.

With a loving God watching over you, and your family and friends taking care of you, you have so much to smile about. So go ahead and do it!

THOUGHT OF THE DAY

If you can't find something to smile about, ask God to give you joy.

PRAY TODAY

Dear God, please help me remember all the good things You have done for me when I'm feeling sad. Amen.

ALL ABOUT ATTITUDE

Though a righteous man falls seven times, he will get up,
but the wicked will stumble into ruin.

Proverbs 24:16 HCSB

I f you're having a little trouble getting something done, don't get mad or frustrated, don't get discouraged, and don't give up. Ask God to help you to keep trying. With His help, you can do some amazing things . . . but if you quit at the first sign of trouble, you might miss out on something great!

THOUGHT OF THE DAY

Everyone falls down, but what matters is getting back up again!

PRAY TODAY

Dear God, when I feel like giving up, help me do the right thing . . . and help me finish what You want me to do. Amen.

AVOIDING MISCHIEF

If you want to stay out of trouble, be careful what you say.

Proverbs 21:23 GNT

Not everybody makes good choices. In fact, you probably have some friends who make bad choices—a lot. Words and actions can cause a lot of problems if you don't watch out. The trick is to avoid the temptation to join in when your friends are causing trouble!

The moment that you decide not to do or say something wrong or hurtful is the moment that you'll make yourself happy, your parents happy, and God happy. You'll also stay out of trouble. Now that's smart!

THOUGHT OF THE DAY

Do you find it hard to resist when your friends tempt you to do something wrong? Practice saying the word "no" out loud. Ask God to help you do the right thing.

PRAY TODAY

Dear God, please help me to stay out of trouble, especially when my friends want me to do something I know is wrong. Amen.

aLways TeLL THe TRUTH

Yes, what joy for those whose record the Lord has cleared of guilt, whose lives are lived in complete honesty!

Psalm 32:2 NLT

Have you ever done something wrong or foolish? Were you tempted to lie about it? Take it from Junior, telling lies to cover up your mistake is not the way to stay out of trouble!

Fibs have a way of getting totally out of control. After a while, it becomes harder and harder to keep track of all of the little lies, and the problem just gets bigger and bigger and bigger!

If you tell a lie, your problem will almost always get a lot worse. Telling the truth–from the start–is the smart way to go.

THOUGHT OF THE DAY

Always tell the truth and you'll never have to worry about what to say!

PRAY TODAY

Dear God, when I make a mistake, I don't want to ever make things worse. Help me to always tell the truth–right away! Amen.

Don't Be in a Hurry

Let your patience show itself perfectly in what you do. Then you will be perfect and complete and will have everything you need.

James 1:4 NCV

When you're in a hurry, you tend to make more mistakes. If you are too quick to do things first and think about the consequences later, you could be sorry for what you've done–maybe right away!

The Bible teaches us that patience can help us in every situation. If we can learn to practice patience each day, God says we will have everything we need.

Usually, the best way to make a wise decision is to slow down long enough to think things through before you act, not after. So, ask God to help you to stop and think first!

THOUGHT OF THE DAY
It's better to be slow-and-safe than fast-and-sorry!

PRAY TODAY
Dear God, help me to slow down today and practice being patient. Amen.

WHEN PEOPLE ARE MEAN

Hatred stirs up trouble, but love forgives all wrongs.

Proverbs 10:12 NCV

It's true—sometimes people can be mean. Really mean. When that happens, your feelings can get hurt and you may be tempted to say something mean back. Don't do it! Instead, remember that God doesn't want you to do what they did. He will take care of other people and their mistakes in His own way.

When people are mean or cruel, remember that God wants you to forgive them the way He has forgiven you. So, when you hear hurtful words, ask God to help you forgive them.

THOUGHT OF THE DAY

Has someone forgiven you for doing something mean or wrong? How did that make you feel?

PRAY TODAY

Dear God, some people can be mean and cruel, but I know that You want me to forgive them right away. Thank You for helping me. Amen.

Practice Self-Control

You must follow the Lord your God and fear Him. You must keep His commands and listen to His voice; you must worship Him and remain faithful to Him.

Deuteronomy 13:4 HCSB

When you learn to control your actions and your words, you will find it easier to obey your parents, your teachers, and even your Father in heaven. Why? Because in order to be an obedient person, you must first learn how to control yourself—otherwise, you won't be able to obey very well, even when you want to.

Learning to control yourself takes lots of practice. God can help us obey Him and to have self-control. Keep trusting God for an obedient heart and for the will to do the right thing.

THOUGHT OF THE DAY

The truth in the Bible is forever. God won't change His mind.

PRAY TODAY

Dear God, I trust You and I know that You want the best for me. Help me to obey You, even when it's hard. Amen.

God's Love is Here to Stay

But for those who honor the Lord, his love lasts forever, and his goodness endures for all generations.

Psalm 103:17 GNT

It's a fact: God loves you. And His love doesn't come and go. Even when you make mistakes or do things that are wrong, His love for you never changes. He loves you all the time, not just some of the time.

When our hearts are filled up with His love, we want to praise Him, thank Him, obey Him and share the Good News of His Son.

Today, pray from your heart and thank Him for His great love for you. Then do your best to honor Him with your good thoughts, kind words, and good deeds.

THOUGHT OF THE DAY
Feelings change all the time, but God never changes.

PRAY TODAY
Dear God, thank You for Your amazing love. You care for me, Father, and I want to make You proud now and forever. Amen.

Big Things

You are young, but do not let anyone treat you as if you were not important. Be an example to show the believers how they should live. Show them with your words, with the way you live, with your love, with your faith, and with your pure life.

1 Timothy 4:12 ICB

Has anyone ever told you that you can't do something important because you are "too young"? Don't believe it! God says you can do anything with Him–no matter how old you are!

You don't have to wait to be a grownup to do something amazing for God. Even small acts of kindness and caring can change someone's life–or the world–forever. And you can have an idea that no one else has ever thought of before. Remember, with God's help, little guys can do big things too!

THOUGHT OF THE DAY

Do you have an idea that could help someone? Maybe your parents can help you figure it out. You can do big things!

PRAY TODAY

Dear God, You said I am important, even though I am young. Help me to do what I can to make a difference every day. Amen.

LET IT GO

Do not remember the past events, pay no attention to things of old. Look, I am about to do something new; even now it is coming. Do you not see it?

Isaiah 43:18-19 HCSB

An important part of learning how to forgive is learning how to get over the things that have happened in the past. What happened yesterday is over. There is no way to go back and change it. But if what happened has made you unhappy, the best thing you can do is ask God to help you let it go.

Are you angry with someone? Have your feelings been hurt? Hopefully, the person that hurt you said they were sorry and tried to make things better. But even if that didn't happen, forgive them and trust God to take care of it. God has new and exciting things for you!

THOUGHT OF THE DAY

Don't live in the past. Nothing new happens there.

PRAY TODAY

Dear God, I don't want to stay angry. Please help me forgive just as You have forgiven me. Amen.

TRUSTING GOD

Trust in the Lord with all your heart, and do not lean on your own understanding.

Proverbs 3:5 ESV

Sometimes, things happen that we simply don't understand. Maybe something didn't work out quite the way you thought it would. Or maybe God wants you to do something that might seem crazy. But one thing is certain—you can always trust His love for you.

The children of Israel sure thought God was crazy when He told them to move into the Promised Land. There were giants and scary people everywhere! But once they all decided to trust God and obey Him, God did exactly what He said He would. He will do the same for you!

THOUGHT OF THE DAY

Can you think of a time when God helped you . . . even if it didn't make sense?

PRAY TODAY

Dear God, Your plans are always perfect, even if they seem strange to me. I will do my best to follow You and do what You ask. Amen.

WATCH OUT FOR GOSSIP

Stop being hateful! Quit trying to fool people, and start being sincere. Don't be jealous or say cruel things about others.

1 Peter 2:1 CEV

D o you know what gossip is? It's when we talk about people who are not around–usually saying mean or unkind things. When we gossip, after a while, the bad things that we say come back to hurt us, and of course they hurt other people, too. That's why the Bible tells us that gossip is wrong.

So if you want to be a kind person and a good friend, don't gossip . . . and don't listen to people who do.

THOUGHT OF THE DAY

Before you speak, ask yourself: "Would I say this if that person were standing here?"

PRAY TODAY

Dear God, help me only say things that are helpful, loving, and kind, not harmful, mean, or rude. Amen.

Keep Praying

Be anxious for nothing, but in everything by prayer and supplication, with thanksgiving, let your requests be made known to God.

Philippians 4:6 NKJV

D o you talk to God about all kinds of things through-out the day? If so, that's great! But if you don't think about praying very often, it might help you to know how much God likes hearing from you.

When something great happens and you are excited, God is excited too! When you are sad, He wants to comfort you. And, when you have choices to make, God wants to help you make the right one.

The more you remember to pray, the closer you are to God. And that's a great thing!

THOUGHT OF THE DAY
What are three things that happened today that you can talk to God about?

PRAY TODAY
Dear God, sometimes I forget to pray. Please help me remember that You are always there for me. Amen.

BE HAPPY FOR OTHERS

Jealousy is more dangerous and cruel than anger.

Proverbs 27:4 TLB

The Bible gives us lots of good advice for how to live our lives. But one thing God thought was so important that He made it one of the Ten Commandments, is that we should not be jealous of other people.

The Bible says that jealousy is worse than anger! We know that anger can cause a lot of hurt and destruction. Imagine what jealousy could do!

The simple solution is to be happy with what you have. When someone you know gets something you like, just be happy for them. Don't waste one moment feeling jealous!

THOUGHT OF THE DAY

God loves to bless you and does all the time. So be happy when He blesses your friends!

PRAY TODAY

Dear God, help me to be happy for others! I will choose to obey You. Amen.

ears to Hear

He who has ears to hear, let him hear.

Matthew 11:15 ESV

Do you like to listen to what your friends have to say? Do you enjoy talking with them and sharing ideas? God feels the same way about you!

God loves to listen when you pray, and He wants you to hear what He has to say, too.

The Bible says that if you have ears to hear, you will hear. You can never hear too much of what God is saying—so pay attention!

THOUGHT OF THE DAY

Hearing God really is just paying attention to what He is saying.

PRAY TODAY

Dear God, thank You for listening to me. I want to hear what You are saying to me, too. Amen.

KIND WORDS

A kind answer soothes angry feelings, but harsh words stir them up.

Proverbs 15:1 CEV

You probably know that God wants you to be kind to others, and there are lots of great ways you can show kindness. But a really important one is the way you speak to people.

There is a lot of power in the words you speak. That comes with great responsibility, but that also means that you can help change any situation for the better by choosing your words carefully.

Try it out! The next time you are angry and tempted to say mean words, try answering with kindness, instead. What happens may surprise you!

THOUGHT OF THE DAY

It can be hard to think when you're angry. So have a good answer ready. Maybe you could try, "I'm sorry you feel that way. How can I make it better?"

PRAY TODAY

Dear God, I know it is really important that I treat others with kindness, so please help me choose my words carefully. Amen.

Using Good Manners

Treat others just as you want to be treated.

Luke 6:31 CEV

Your parents have probably spent a lot of time teaching you about using good manners. They do that because the way you act when you are around other people does two things—it changes what people think about you, and also how they will treat you.

Nobody likes rude manners or unkind words. Using good manners like saying "please," "thank you," and "excuse me" are just the beginning, and if you always act with kindness and thoughtfulness, others will usually treat you the same way.

THOUGHT OF THE DAY

What do you like better—when others are rude or kind to you?

PRAY TODAY

Dear God, please help me remember to use good manners all the time. Amen.

WHO YOU ARE

And if children, then heirs–heirs of God and fellow heirs with Christ.

Romans 8:17 ESV

D o you know who you are? You probably know your name, the people in your family, and where you live. But you are so much more than that!

If you love Jesus, that makes you God's child! That means you are part of God's family. You have everything Jesus does. You are made in God's image! You are loved and cherished by God.

Don't let anyone tell you differently–you are special!

THOUGHT OF THE DAY

God made only one you!

PRAY TODAY

Dear God, I am so glad to belong to You. Thank You for making me and loving me just the way I am. Amen.

Share What You Have

Do not neglect to do good and to share what you have, for such sacrifices are pleasing to God.

Hebrews 13:16 ESV

When you were little, did you share your toys and your snacks with your friends? Hopefully! Fortunately you are a lot bigger now, and you have more wonderful things to offer.

God doesn't expect you to give something you don't have, or can't get. He only wants you to be willing to freely share what you do have. Whether that is a favorite toy or just a smile, do what you can do, and God will be really pleased.

THOUGHT OF THE DAY
Sharing can be the best part of your day!

PRAY TODAY
Dear God, I may not be able to share everything that people need, but help me to share what I do have. Amen.

Strong and Courageous

"Have I not commanded you? Be strong and courageous. Do not be frightened, and do not be dismayed, for the Lord your God is with you wherever you go."

Joshua 1:9 ESV

Almost all of the great men and women in the Bible have one thing in common . . . when the time came to obey God, they all chose to be strong, have courage, and trust Him.

You are no different! God promised to never leave them, and He has promised to never leave you. He is with you everywhere you go, in every situation. So don't give up. Instead, be strong and courageous and trust God!

God has great things ahead for you!

THOUGHT OF THE DAY
Don't ever be afraid to try. God will help you!

PRAY TODAY
Dear God, thank You for helping me be strong and courageous today. Amen.

GOD LOVES YOU VERY MUCH

But God showed how much he loved us by having Christ die for us, even though we were sinful.

Romans 5:8 CEV

The whole Bible is really the story of how much God loves you! It's true!

Thousands of years before you were born, God was thinking about you. When He created the Earth and made Adam and Eve, even then you were on His mind. When He sent Jesus to die for the whole world, He wanted to save you.

That's a pretty big thing to understand, and God will help you all your life to understand Him and His love more every day.

THOUGHT OF THE DAY

Nobody knows you like God does, and no one can match His love for you.

PRAY TODAY

Dear God, thank You for loving me so much. I can't understand it, but I know it's true. Amen.

GROWING UP

We make our own plans, but the Lord decides where we will go.

Proverbs 16:9 CEV

You are growing and changing and experiencing a lot of new things. That's pretty exciting! And no one is happier about how you are growing than God.

The good news is you can work hard on whatever challenge is next, because you know He loves you and is there to guide your steps.

THOUGHT OF THE DAY

What new things do you want to try and do next?

PRAY TODAY

Dear God, thank You for all the plans You have made for me and for making sure I go in the right direction. Amen.

Praise Him all Day

My mouth is filled with your praise, and with your glory all the day.

Psalm 71:8 ESV

If you love God and know how much He loves you, you might find yourself wanting to speak, sing, and even pray wonderful and special things about Him all the time.

Praising God is one of the best things you can do. Not only does it make God's heart glad, but it will make your heart happy, too.

That's a really good reason to keep your heart full of praise for God all the time. It will fill your days with joy and gladness, and make you want to dance and sing!

THOUGHT OF THE DAY

Read the book of Psalms in the Bible with your parents. It is packed full of praise for God!

PRAY TODAY

Dear God, thank You for being who You are and for everything You have done for me. I am so thankful. Amen.

Mom or Dad, talk to your son about what this verse means
and help him memorize this verse . . .

*Those who are pure in their thinking
are happy, because
they will be with God.*

Matthew 5:8 NCV

Mom or Dad, talk to your son about what this verse means
and help him memorize this verse . . .

*This is the day which the LORD has made;
let us rejoice and be glad in it.*

–

Psalm 118:24 NASB

KNOW IT BY HEART

Mom or Dad, talk to your son about what this verse means
and help him memorize this verse . . .

*Be of good courage,
and He shall strengthen your heart,
all you who hope in the Lord.*

-

Psalm 31:24 NKJV

KNOW IT BY HEART

Mom or Dad, talk to your son about what this verse means
and help him memorize this verse . . .

*For God so loved the world that
he gave his one and only Son,
that whoever believes in him
shall not perish but have eternal life.*

John 3:16 NIV

Mom or Dad, talk to your son about what this verse means
and help him memorize this verse . . .

Trust in the LORD with all your heart;
do not depend on your own understanding.
Seek his will in all you do,
and he will direct your paths.

Proverbs 3:5-6 NLT

Mom or Dad, talk to your son about what this verse means
and help him memorize this verse . . .

*I came that they may have life,
and have it abundantly.*

–

John 10:10 NASB

Mom or Dad, talk to your son about what this verse means
and help him memorize this verse . . .

*To everything there is a season,
a time for every purpose under heaven.*

—

Ecclesiastes 3:1 NKJV

Mom or Dad, talk to your son about what this verse means
and help him memorize this verse . . .

*Above all else, guard your heart,
for it affects everything you do.*

Proverbs 4:23 NLT

Mom or Dad, talk to your son about what this verse means
and help him memorize this verse . . .

*I tell you the truth, anything you did
for even the least of my people here,
you also did for me.*

Matthew 25:40 NCV

KNOW IT BY HEART

Mom or Dad, talk to your son about what this verse means
and help him memorize this verse . . .

*My cup runs over.
Surely goodness and mercy
shall follow me all the days of my life;
and I will dwell in the house
of the Lord forever.*

Psalm 23:5-6 NKJV

Mom or Dad, talk to your son about what this verse means
and help him memorize this verse . . .

*So these three things continue forever:
faith, hope, and love.
And the greatest of these is love.*

1 Corinthians 13:13 ICB